Toxic Workplace!

Toxic Workplace!

Managing Toxic Personalities and Their Systems of Power

Mitchell E. Kusy
and Elizabeth L. Holloway

JOSSEY-BASS
A Wiley Imprint
www.josseybass.com

Published by Jossey-Bass
A Wiley Imprint
989 Market Street, San Francisco, CA 94103-1741—www.josseybass.com

Library of Congress Cataloging-in-Publication Data

Kusy, Mitchell.
   Toxic workplace! : managing toxic personalities and their systems of power / Mitchell E. Kusy and Elizabeth L. Holloway.
   — 1st ed.
      p. cm.
   Includes bibliographical references and index.
   ISBN 978-0-470-42484-1 (cloth)
   1. Problem employees. 2. Interpersonal conflict. 3. Conflict management. 4. Personnel management. I. Holloway, Elizabeth. II. Title.
   HF5549.5.E42K87 2009
   658.3'045—dc22

                                                                        2008055671

Printed in the United States of America

FIRST EDITION

HB Printing   10

Contents

To all those who have suffered from the effects of toxic behaviors at work. And to the leaders who told us their stories in hope of finding paths to respectful engagement in their organizations and communities.

Toxic Workplace!

"The day this person left our organization is considered an annual holiday!"

Part One

Understanding Toxic People and Toxic Environments

Before you can solve a problem, you have to fully understand it. Therefore, the chapters in Part One examine in depth toxic people—those who do damage to their coworkers, staffs, bosses, and customers. Chapter One describes the significant organizational losses, human and financial, that these people cause. Because recognizing toxicity is not easy, Chapter Two describes the types of toxic behavior, from humiliating others to sabotaging team efforts. Chapter Three identifies strategies that *don't* work in dealing with toxic people so you won't waste your time on these! And Chapter Four shows how toxicity spreads like an infection in organizations.

1

THE HUMAN AND FINANCIAL COSTS OF WORKING WITH TOXIC PEOPLE

Toxic Behaviors Are Just the Tip of the Iceberg

Working with this toxic individual was one of the worst experiences in my life. It took a long time to recover from her abuse. It was difficult because others witnessed what was happening but were scared they might receive the same abuse so they did not want to get involved.

—*Quote from study respondent*

You have probably picked up this book because you are either suffering or have suffered the ravages of a toxic personality at work. Most people have. Does the opening quotation from our national study on toxic personalities, in which we interviewed and surveyed more than four hundred leaders, hit close to home? Maybe it resurrects memories of your own gut-wrenching experiences with toxic personalities at work

Most of us have experienced the frustration and confusion of having an extremely difficult person to deal with in the workplace. Call them what you will: *control freaks, narcissists, manipulators, bullies, poisonous individuals,* or *humiliators,* to name just a few of the descriptors that we heard during our interviews. And we have heard other terms in our consulting practices and our research that describe what these people do: *poison, corrupt, pollute,* and *contaminate.* This is not your common, everyday variety of difficult person who gets on your nerves occasionally but without lasting effects. Instead, based on our research, we define the toxic personality as anyone who demonstrates a pattern of counterproductive work behaviors that debilitate individuals, teams, and even organizations over the long term.

> Based on our research, we define the toxic personality as anyone who demonstrates a pattern of counterproductive work behaviors that debilitate individuals, teams, and even organizations over the long term.

These difficult individuals have the capacity to pervade our thoughts and sap our energies so much so that they have the potential to undermine our sense of well-being. In a variety of ways, they get under our skin, infiltrate our professional and personal space, demoralize us, demotivate teams, and ultimately can even make us doubt our own competence and productivity. They are toxic in every sense of the term.

In the most egregious situations, we may have an exaggerated emotional reaction to their toxicity and carry these feelings home to our families, friends, and significant others. These reactions may include lashing out at others, being uncommunicative about what is eating away at us, and even being in a significant depression requiring medication. Unfortunately, unless you can pick up and move to a new job, it seems impossible to escape the deleterious effects of these toxic individuals. And sometimes these effects continue even after the toxic person is no longer around. We found many situations where the toxicity lingers in the system after the toxic person leaves voluntarily or is fired.

> In the most egregious situations, we may have an exaggerated emotional reaction to their toxicity and carry these feelings home to our families, friends, and significant others.

The Ubiquity of Toxic People

How pervasive is this problem? In our survey results, 64 percent of the respondents were currently working with a toxic personality, and a whopping 94 percent have worked with someone toxic in their career. Another research study discovered that 27 percent of employees in a representative sample of seven hundred Michigan residents experienced mistreatment by someone at work.[1] And in certain occupations, the abuse is astronomical. For example, in a study of nurses, an overwhelming 91 percent had experienced verbal abuse, defined as mistreatment in which they felt attacked, devalued, or humiliated; in addition, more than 50 percent did not believe themselves competent to respond to the verbal abuse.[2] In general, one study after another confirms that verbal abuse increases job dissatisfaction, builds a hostile work setting, and lowers morale.

Here's another example. In an ingenious and clever study, employees in a manufacturing plant carried handheld computers for up to three weeks.[3] At four random intervals daily, they had to report any interactions with either a coworker or boss from the perspective of whether the interaction was positive or negative and what their current mood was at the time. The researchers found that the negative interactions affected the moods of these employees five times more strongly than the positive ones, even though they reported positive interactions three to five times more often than the negative ones.

To get a further sense of the intensity of these interactions, author Robert Sutton described the effects of "jerks" in the workplace.[4] He identified a situation in which a CEO of a health care information technology system company, sent an e-mail he had intended for the organization's highest-level folks. In this message, he bemoaned the fact that not all employees were working full forty-hour weeks and said he wanted the employee parking lot full from 7:30 A.M. to 6:30 P.M. on weekdays and half full on Saturdays. If management couldn't do this within the next two weeks, he said he'd take harsh measures.

As you may have guessed, word leaked out about this message on the Internet. After investors saw this, *the company's stock fell 22 percent in three days!* With an apology the CEO sent to his employees, the share price returned to normal. We relate this story because it demonstrates the effects that just one uncivil demand can have on others *and* the organization. We don't believe Sutton was necessarily saying that the CEO was toxic. But if a single isolated behavior of the CEO has this effect on an organization, imagine the ripple effects that can occur with ongoing toxic behaviors over the long term.

Why We Wrote This Book

In our consulting work in the areas of organization development, leadership development, team development, and coaching, we have had many clients voice their problems with toxic people. At a loss for what to do, they recounted the devastation this has caused—both the financial and human costs of the toxic person's effects on others.

To get to the root of this evasive and pervasive problem, we conducted a two-year research study on the prevalence and effects of toxicity in organizations. This book contains the results of that research and has helped our clients create more effective communities in their organizations defined by respectful engagement. This book offers you ways to manage existing toxic behaviors and create norms that prevent the growth (or regrowth) of toxic environments.

We have talked with our clients about the subtle and not-so-subtle difficulties that toxic personalities create in their organizations. These are just a few of the many questions our clients have posed to us in our work with toxic personalities:

- Who are these toxic individuals?
- What makes them tick?

- How do they survive in organizations?
- Why are their poisonous behaviors allowed to continue for so long?
- Why are the effects they have on others so consuming?
- Where do they get their support?
- How should leaders best handle them for maximum benefit to the organization?
- What if the leader is toxic?
- How do we stop them in their tracks? Can we?
- What needs to occur so that the organizational community operates through respectful engagement?

The answers are not simple, but they do translate into courses of action that can make a difference between success and failure in dealing with a toxic person and their environment.

How We Researched the Problem of Toxic Personalities at Work

Our first step in understanding the problem of toxic personalities in organizations and seeking solutions was to design a research study that would ask successful leaders who had encountered these individuals to tell us their stories. We wanted to know the details of what happened in their organizations, teams, and relationships when they worked with a toxic person. We did not want to focus merely on the identified problem—that is, the toxic individual. Rather, we wanted to understand everything that was happening around this person. Essentially, we studied both the toxic person *and* the associated system. It was our premise as seasoned therapists and consultants that understanding the whole system would give us a better view of how leaders can build strategies for dealing with these extremely difficult people.

We used both interviews and surveys to gain information from more than four hundred successful leaders—CEOs, executives, managers, team leaders, supervisors, project managers, and directors—at both for-profit companies and nonprofit organizations. Interviews are important because they reveal the intricacies and subtle nuances of a problem by providing unencumbered expressions of actual experiences. Surveys are equally significant because they provide a rich source of quantitative data from which to make extrapolations of meaningful correlations between key factors.

Our research study had three phases (see Appendix A for details on the survey):

Phase 1: Informal, unstructured interviews with fifty "thought leaders"—individuals from our consulting network who were reflective and direct about the many issues facing their organizations

Phase 2: Formal interviews with fifteen leaders from the profit and nonprofit sectors

Phase 3: An eighty-two-item survey of 962 leaders, with responses from approximately 400

Our interviews identified five areas of importance that we used to construct the survey:

- The toxic person's characteristics and behaviors
- Leaders' reactions to toxic behaviors
- Leaders' strategies for dealing with the toxic person
- Effects of toxicity on the system
- The role of organizational culture on toxicity

We wanted to understand the degree of toxicity leaders experienced. To do this, we asked them to consider one individual whom they regarded as toxic. Then we requested that they rate the intensity of this individual's toxicity on a scale from 1 to 10, with the greatest toxicity they could imagine being 10. Figure 1.1 illustrates that 74 percent rated the problem person's toxicity

Figure 1.1 Level of Toxicity Reported by Leaders in Our Study

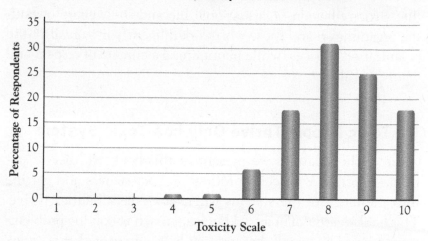

Note: Toxicity was measured on a scale of 1 to 10, with 10 being the highest degree of toxicity.

from 8 to 10 and 92 percent from 7 to 10. We interpreted this finding to mean that the intensity of toxic behavior that almost all of our respondents experienced was very high. In addition, approximately 90 percent of these leaders reported that the person they identified exhibited toxic behaviors anywhere from two to five times per week.

We note that our respondents named males and females alike in this group; there were no significant differences in gender of toxic individuals. And to answer the next question that may be on your mind, 65 percent of our respondents were female and 35 percent were male.

These descriptive statistics on the degree of toxicity distinguish between difficult behavior that occurs for almost everyone on a bad day and habitual behaviors that are part of a person's style of engaging with others. In psychological language, it is these individuals' *interpersonal style* that is problematic. They have been using problematic behaviors for years to get what they need from others. Notice our use of "get what they need" rather than what others in the organization need or what the organization itself needs. Our focus in this book is on the insidious effects that toxicity has on organizational life and the welfare of both the organization and those who work diligently in pursuit of the organization's success while maintaining a climate of respect and dignity for all.

Toxic People Thrive Only in a Toxic System

Some of the solutions we present in this book are easy to put in place; others will require rolling up your sleeves and getting into the muck of the systems where toxic personalities thrive. This book doesn't offer a cookbook approach to solving problems caused by toxic people because we have discovered that quick recipes don't work: toxic personalities are part of a complex system, which is the source of their power. Therefore, a solid grounding in systems dynamics is required to combat their hold on the organization.

Once you understand how these people derive power from the systems, you'll be prepared to make a critical difference in how your organization, team, or community deals with them. Notice that we say "your organization, team, or community." This is intentional, because although the leader is certainly a key player in this dimension, the leader will not be able to intervene as effectively without your help in understanding the system dynamics of the toxic situation.

Many leaders who responded to our study were caught in the complex web of toxicity and weren't often able to extricate themselves. This web is what we refer to as a *toxic system*. It is a system because the most critical element of understanding how to change toxicity is to view it from a dynamic interactive perspective. A toxic person's behaviors trigger reactions from others. Soon the triggers and the reactions begin to damage the team or individuals, who may react in ways that actually reinforce the toxic behaviors. Simply intervening with the toxic person is not effective because others may have learned new ways of interacting that are largely in response to the toxic triggers. Toxic personalities are part of a complex system, which is the source of their power. Therefore, a solid grounding in systems dynamics is required to combat their hold on the organization.

The responsibility for dealing with the toxic persons effectively shifts to the system as a whole. Addressing the system is the only way we have discovered to handle the problem effectively and inoculate the organization from further damage. We call our systems approach the *toxic organization change system* (TOCS), because it's the system that becomes the first call to action. Our TOCS model helps leaders identify and produce the most effective systemwide change in workplace toxicity through three change strategies: organization (which we discuss in Chapter Five), team (which we discuss in Chapter Six), and individual (which we discuss in Chapter Seven).

Our TOCS model helps leaders identify and produce the most effective systemwide change in workplace toxicity through three change strategies: organization, team, and individual.

To date, there have been few empirical studies dealing with the practical components of how leaders can mitigate the significant human and financial costs of toxic individuals. Toxicity spreads in systems with long-term effects on organizational climate even after the person has left voluntarily or has been dismissed. To discourage this spread, we provide *reactive* measures. To encourage environments where toxic individuals would find it difficult to be hired or survive, we provide *proactive* approaches. Both deal with the system components of toxicity. First, only when the system around which the toxic personality functions is identified can meaningful change take effect. Second, once this systemic change occurs, only then will one-on-one interventions with the toxic personality become more effective.

Only when the system around which the toxic personality functions is identified can meaningful change take effect. Once this systemic change occurs, only then will one-on-one interventions with the toxic personality become more effective.

This book calls for not only managing toxicity interpersonally but also for managing the system within which they operate. *Toxic Workplace!* describes specific interventions needed to stop toxic people in their tracks, and it will help you manage system change so that no toxic individual in the organization can flourish.

The Hidden Chunk of the Toxic Iceberg

Although we regard the tip of the iceberg as the toxic individual, what is crucial to understand is the impact of this toxic iceberg on the organization—the human and financial costs of toxic behavior (see Figure 1.2). These have long been hidden from the direct-line view of many leaders and nonleaders alike—below the waterline, if you will. Some of the statistics we present may surprise you especially because it has taken so long to do something about this ubiquitous issue that is prevalent in all kinds of organizations. In fact, we found no differences in incidence of toxicity or leader strategies between profit and nonprofit organizations. Although the following studies are not focused on what leaders specifically need to do, they do provide excellent cues in better understanding how toxic individuals burden people and organizational systems.

Figure 1.2 The Tip of the Toxic Iceberg

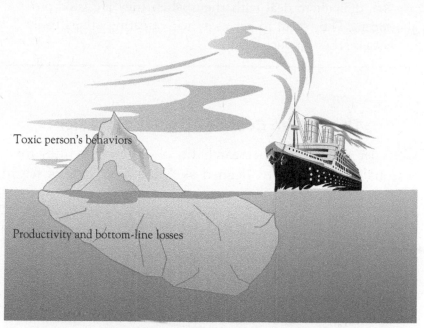

Toxic person's behaviors

Productivity and bottom-line losses

For example, one large-scale research study[5] of fifty-one manufacturing teams and another study[6] both revealed that a team member who was rated low on interpersonal traits decreased the entire team's performance significantly. In other words, the team is only as strong as its weakest link.

In our consulting practices, people have asked us, "Don't leaders see what this person is doing to the team?" Sometimes they do; sometimes they don't. And when they do, there may be reasons for not acting. For example, one leader in our study reported, "It's difficult to deal with them when they are good producers. They seem to get away with treating others badly because they produce results." And another noted: "Management was passive about the behavior because this person produced work that was viewed as good."

But as you'll soon see, producing results is just one gain in a whole constellation of negative effects that can bring the entire organization down.

"It's difficult to deal with them when they are good producers. They seem to get away with treating others badly because they produce results."

The Hidden Costs of Uncivil Behavior

Consider the results of research on one domain within toxic personalities—incivility, defined as "employees' lack of regard for one another":[7]

- Almost 50 percent of those who experienced incivility at work reported that they lost time worrying about this and its future consequences.
- More than 25 percent of individuals who were targets of incivility acknowledged that they cut back their work efforts.
- Fifty percent contemplated leaving their jobs after being the target of incivility, and 12 percent actually did so.[8]

In our own study, one leader related how significant turnover costs can be:

> This toxic person is in the most senior HR leadership role in the organization. He has experienced 80 percent turnover of his direct reporting team and staff [as a result of his toxicity].

In a subsequent study of eight hundred employees:[9]

- Twenty percent stated they were targets of incivility at least once a week.
- Ten percent said they witnessed incivility daily at work.

The Hidden Costs of Bullying

One specific arena of incivility is *bullying*, defined as someone who places targets in a submissive, powerless position whereby they are more easily influenced and controlled, in order to achieve personal or organizational objectives.[10] When someone cuts a path of destruction with bullying behaviors, the organization sees higher turnover, less favorable attitudes toward the job and the organization, and greater psychological distress than as experienced with nonbullies.[11] Bullying, in fact, has increased over the past several decades.[12] One explanation for this increase is that organizations are running flatter and leaner, with fewer management structures in place to corral bullies.

How Human Resource Professionals View Toxicity

It appears that no one is immune to the ravages of toxic personalities, not even human resource (HR) professionals, whom we initially thought might have the edge on working with toxic individuals. In our study, even they could not put their fingers on effective methods. These professionals need strategies that deal with toxic personalities for both their internal clients and themselves, because they are as affected by toxic individuals as anyone else. Human resource professionals had some interesting insights about toxic persons. In one study of HR work teams,[13] researchers found that the lowest member's score for conscientiousness and agreeableness predicts group performance and does so over and above cognitive ability. So according to HR professionals, intelligence is not as good a predictor of a team's success as conscientiousness and agreeableness are.

When you interview potential team members, how much time do you spend trying to determine the applicant's fit with the team? Typically leaders spend an inordinate amount of time on the content of the team's work—such factors as expertise, education, and work on similar projects. We're not saying these aren't important. What we *are* saying (based on these research studies) is that you need to spend time on more subtle personality factors when recruiting individuals and team members.

The research on emotional intelligence supports the position that fit plays a critical role in both individual and team success. Emotional intelligence exemplifies the ability to understand your own feelings as well as the feelings of others—a quality often lacking in some of the toxic individuals we heard about in our study. Emotional intelligence experts label the understanding of one's own feelings as "personal competence," which incorporates the dimensions of self-awareness and self-management. In our study, we found that these two factors are sometimes lacking in toxic individuals.

The second big arena in emotional intelligence is social competence, which encompasses social awareness and relationship management, both deficient in many toxic folks. Because toxic individuals lack some of the more important dimensions of emotional intelligence and there are hundreds of documented studies linking emotional intelligence to success, many toxic individuals detract from organizational success. Some toxic individuals are successful in their jobs, but they are usually not successful when they are evaluated against their paths of destruction. Consider the toll they take when employees leave the organization or do not want to work with them. Even customers and other key stakeholders say they'd rather work with someone else in the organization or, worse, go elsewhere for their customer needs. Toxic people leave a significant debris field. Here's one in particular from our research study: "They tend to pollute the environment with their negativity, and I have seen others quit at a previous organization as a result of their behavior."

Turnover is an ever-present problem with victims of toxic personalities. When you consider that the fully loaded costs of turnover are anywhere from one and a half to two and a half times the salary paid for the job, you can see the tremendous financial impact of the toxic person, along with the human suffering and loss.[14]

Some toxic individuals are successful in their jobs, but they are usually not successful when they are evaluated against their paths of destruction.

How Do Toxic People Get Hired in the First Place?

Our research sent us on a saga to truly understand this widespread and recalcitrant problem that undermines the health of organizations and people. The consulting we have done in this arena has served as a robust laboratory for experimenting with the benchmarked practices we discovered in our research study. Many leaders asked, "Can't personality tests address this problem by weeding out toxic individuals from ever entering organizations?" Our best answer is, "to a limited extent." There's a fair amount of research evidence that personality tests can predict an individual's performance reasonably well. And there's even evidence that personality tests can predict factors such as how conscientious someone is likely to be, how agreeable during times of conflict, and even how emotionally stable the person is. However, the counterproductive behaviors addressed in these tests are overt actions, such as fighting, stealing, and absenteeism. Although those behaviors are clearly undesirable, these are not the toxic behaviors we addressed in our study. Ours are much more subtle than these direct acts of aggression, but they are just as problematic to people and organizations.

Why Not Just Fire Toxic People?

You may be asking yourself (or us!), "Why not just fire them?" Firing certainly is appropriate in many circumstances. But there are two reasons that this does not occur as often as it should. First, the leader may not have gone through an effective performance management process with this individual, as most organizations require. Second, in some organizations, this process is not well delineated, there may not be HR support to work with the leader, or no one knows how to work with these behaviors. In addition, the process just takes too long in some organizations. As one of our respondents noted, "It was just too draining to go through the process of firing them."

Finally, how do you fire someone who is an effective employee in that he or she meets the standards of the job (or even exceeds them)? Based on our study, we have found that the organization values need to be absolutely concrete and behaviorally specific, as well as integrated into existing performance management systems. Subsequently, living out the values becomes just as "real" in terms of appraisal of performance as the day-to-day tasks one has to do. And since most organizations don't have these kinds of values that become a key factor associated with one's job, firing is even more difficult.

Beware the "Bad Apple" Effect of Toxic Behavior

Consider what is often referred to in the psychological and management literature as the *bad apple syndrome*. This has been corroborated by other researchers who found that a team made up of two emotionally unstable and two stable members performed as badly as a group of all unstable members![15] It's almost as if the emotionally unstable team member infects the rest of the team with negative energy.[16] They found that negative relationships have a greater impact on job satisfaction and organizational commitment than do neutral or even positive relationships. For example, one leader in our study related how disastrous this was to the personal psyche of so many: "Her behavior was so extreme that people were almost immobilized."

"It was just too draining to go through the process of firing them." It is not uncommon for many of us to look for a new position in response to a boss or colleague who is toxic in every sense of the term. You may have experienced, or can imagine, the emotional toll this problem creates in organizations and how this emotional strain plays out in organizational productivity.

All of these studies dramatically expose the importance of examining the effects of and the solutions for dealing with toxic forces in your organization. Two of our respondents summed up the significantly negative effects of just one toxic individual:

> The amount of impact of toxic people is a cost that ripples through the organization. It has tentacles that few have measured. If one could ever show the wide-reaching effects of just ONE toxic person, I think it would help people address this sooner.

> Talented people left the organization; marginal performers are the ones who stayed.

There are both overt and sometimes subtle effects of the toxic person, which is why we use the metaphor of the tip of the iceberg. Although you can see the toxic person at the surface, the insidious effects the toxic person has on the organizational system are well below the surface.

Summing Up

We hope you're now ready to delve more deeply into the world of the toxic personality. *World* is an appropriate word here because it indicates the system around which the toxic individual thrives. We have provided you with a big picture perspective of this system with a glimpse of what the bottom part of the iceberg looks like in a toxic system. In the following chapters, you will examine hands-on approaches to understand the toxic system and the toxic individual by completing portions of the same survey that respondents did in our national study, as well as seeing the detailed results of our research. These results have clear implications for how leaders lead, how organizational cultures sustain them, and how teams deal with toxic personalities.

Chapter Two begins by revealing how to identify toxic individuals. It isn't always easy because some toxic behaviors, even highly damaging ones, can be subtle and insidious.

2

RECOGNIZING THE TOXIC PERSONALITY

It Isn't as Easy as You Think

This person can be quite charismatic and funny, so it is easy to get sucked in time and time again and give her the benefit of the doubt. She has a knack for always asking for forgiveness while still belittling the person. I've decided over the years that she is essentially a manipulative, power-hungry, dishonest, unethical game player. She is not someone I can trust in any situation. She puts people in positions where they feel that they are going against one another, and she does it simply for her own self-interests. She makes it look like she strives for calmness, but in reality seems to get pure enjoyment out of chaos and anxiety-producing situations.

—Quote from study respondent

This quotation from a leader in our study denotes the sheer exasperation he felt in dealing with this toxic individual. How would you like to work with this person? Or maybe you already do.

Understanding the pattern of toxic behaviors in your organizational system is the first step in implementing long-lasting change. Many books on toxic personalities in the workplace create typologies to classify the different ways in which toxic behaviors cause trouble in the work environment. Professional psychologists have diagnostic systems that label individuals who have certain patterns of behavior that they use consistently. However, you do not need to memorize labels and syndromes to recognize how toxic behaviors are affecting your work and the work of those around you.

A tip in recognizing toxicity is that there may be (and likely are) different perspectives about the toxic person; there may even be some people who do not experience the person's toxicity at all. This is especially true for those who are in a position of power or control access to powerful others, perks, or any number of resources the toxic individual wants. One respondent reminded us:

> Peers want nothing to do with the person and roll their eyes when they are told they need to include this person in a meeting or other event ... [yet the] direct supervisor of this person isn't always aware of how truly toxic the person is because they put on such a good show when they need to.

So, you need to be vigilant in recognizing that toxic people may act differently when power differentials are present, especially when rewards enter the equation.

Remember that toxic people are adept at masking the toxicity when it is to their advantage. They can turn their behaviors on and off depending on the impression they want to make on the boss, a direct report, a peer, or a customer. As a leader, recognizing that you have a toxicity problem in your team or group means understanding that complaints to you may not be consistent with your impression. Nonetheless, they are accurate renditions of team members' day-to-day experiences. Recognizing the signs of toxicity has important implications for proactive change strategies (which we discuss in detail in Chapters Five, Six, and Seven).

The toxic person is very adept at masking the toxicity when it is to his or her advantage.

What toxic behaviors did we find to be most destructive to individuals, teams, and organizations? How did we go about identifying these behaviors in our study?

Three Types of Toxic Behaviors That Drive People to Distraction

The vast number of intense and revealing comments we received in our survey was a strong indication of the pain our respondents have endured. This was evident to us not only in the seventy-two pages of single-spaced comments we received from survey respondents, but also in the three hundred pages of transcribed text from our in-depth interviews. Many times it was difficult to end our interviews because our respondents wanted finally to tell their stories in complete detail. And many had not previously recounted their ordeal to anyone outside their family and friends.

To help you get a flavor for how the participants in our study experienced the survey, we invite you to complete the first section of it, shown in Exhibit 2.1, which pertains to the twelve toxic behaviors that were most significant from our statistical analysis.

You can then compare your responses with those of leaders in our survey, provided in Appendix B (Tables B.1, B.2, Figure B.1). This comparison will give you a better understanding of the survey responses in total, as well as how you either align or differ from the sample population. Don't be alarmed if your responses are divergent from the comparison group; this just means you have a different view. However, we believe there is a high probability that many of your responses will be similar because there was little variance in the ratings of the toxic behaviors by the four hundred participants in our sample.

Exhibit 2.1 National Survey of Toxic Personalities: Toxic Behaviors

Please consider a toxic person with whom you are working now or with whom you have worked in the past. In your experience with this toxic person, how characteristic of him or her are the following behaviors?

1 = Definitely not at all characteristic of this person
2 = Very little characteristic of this person
3 = A little characteristic of this person
4 = Somewhat characteristic of this person
5 = Mostly characteristic of this person
6 = Definitely characteristic of this person

1. Humiliates others	1 2 3 4 5 6
2. Uses sarcastic remarks	1 2 3 4 5 6
3. Takes "potshots" at others in public	1 2 3 4 5 6
4. Distrusts opinions of others	1 2 3 4 5 6
5. Monitors team behaviors to the point of surveillance	1 2 3 4 5 6
6. Meddles in teamwork	1 2 3 4 5 6
7. Uses authority to punish others	1 2 3 4 5 6
8. Demonstrates passive-aggressive behaviors	1 2 3 4 5 6
9. Protects one's own territory	1 2 3 4 5 6
10. Has difficulty accepting negative feedback	1 2 3 4 5 6
11. Is clueless that they are toxic to others	1 2 3 4 5 6
12. Points out the mistakes of others	1 2 3 4 5 6

Take a look at Appendix B (Table B.1), and then review your responses in light of the results we discuss in this chapter. In this manner, you can determine which behaviors are most relevant to your situation. And remember that even if you haven't encountered some of these toxic behaviors doesn't mean you won't in the future. We would like you to be prepared!

Where did you score higher than our sample population? Lower? Any insights in comparing your responses to theirs? Our motivation in having you do this exercise is to help you better reflect on what this toxicity has personally meant to you. By examining the responses from our sample population, we were able to determine which behaviors were generally endorsed as problematic by a majority of the respondents.

Our first run at the data was to calculate descriptive statistics on each of the twelve behaviors from our research. Questions asked respondents whether the behavior was characteristic of the toxic person that they were describing. You can see in Figure 2.1 a sample of the results from question 9, in which 69 percent of respondents indicated that toxic persons "definitely" protect their own territory and 89 percent endorsed this characteristic as "mostly or definitely characteristic" of this person.

When we examined the behavioral items statistically, we arrived at three primary types of behaviors that put a frame around how to identify them in a simple and straightforward fashion: shaming, passive hostility, and team sabotage (Figure 2.2). The twelve items in Exhibit 2.1 contributed to those three types.

Figure 2.1 Percentage of Toxic People Who Protect Their Own Territory

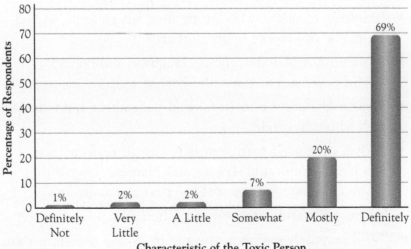

Figure 2.2 The Three Types
of Toxic Behavior

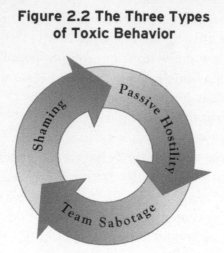

Type 1: Shaming Behavior

Respondents identified the following behaviors as shaming: humiliation, sarcasm, potshots, and mistake pointing. Read the following list of quotations about these behaviors, then consider what these behaviors look like and how they affect workers:

- "Rallies the troops and singles out one person for attack—very nasty and immature behavior."
- "Insulting to others who are treating his patients, including public displays of angry outbursts."
- "Uses arrogant/condescending language and behavior toward peers and at times the boss as well."
- "Sends slanderous e-mails far and wide about individuals with whom he works."
- "When displeased with your behavior or performance, acts like a parent and shames and blames, along with severe emotional swings and even temper tantrums."
- "Demeaning and derogatory to others."
- "Will purposely embarrass people by asking questions that they know these people don't have the answer for."

These descriptions helped us understand how debilitating and yet commonplace it was for leaders and coworkers to put up with abusive, shaming behaviors. There is significant literature on the abusive personality in the workplace and the traumatizing that occurs with shaming and, when power is typically involved, bullying behaviors. In fact, this level of outward physical intimidation and aggression is now protected by policies of harassment and incivility in many organizations.

Some of our respondents referred to outward intimidation, but more prevalent were the insidious verbal humiliations and put-downs that are harder to put a finger on. These start at the irritation stage and become demoralizing as the abuse accumulates day after day. They create an undercurrent of disrespect and negativity long before any active bullying and intimidation might occur. The subtlety of shaming makes it difficult to establish legal and ethical policies around verbal hostility because it is often justified as "just giving feedback or constructive criticism" to someone.

It is no wonder that most leaders wait until the behaviors become so prevalent, obvious, and destructive that they cannot be ignored. Of course, by then, the work unit is poisoned, coworkers are demoralized, and managers feel powerless to change the course of events. We discuss these effects in much greater detail in Chapter Five, but for now, we offer this important comment: not all aggression meets the legal threshold of abuse, but it is nevertheless hostile behavior that has significant effects on the receiver's self-esteem and well-being, as well as the organization's approach to creating a respectful environment.

Not all aggression meets the legal threshold of abuse, but it is nevertheless hostile behavior that has significant effects on the receiver's self-esteem and well-being, as well as the organization's approach to creating a respectful environment.

Type 2: Passive Hostility

The behaviors from our research that were associated with passive hostility are passive aggression, distrust of others' opinions, territorial behavior, verbal attacks when receiving negative feedback, and being clueless of their own toxicity. These behaviors are a little more difficult to spot immediately unless, of course, you live or have lived with someone who is expert in this style of aggression. In this case, you might see the fire before anyone else even smells the smoke. Let's take a look at each of these in more detail.

Toxic People Are Often Passive-Aggressive. Several of the behaviors listed under passive hostility are ones that you will recognize because they are commonly seen as passive-aggressive. And you'll notice in the survey you completed in Exhibit 2.1 that passive aggression is listed because it kept turning up in our in-depth interviews. People who are passive-aggressive often know exactly what the behaviors are in which they are engaging. It is aggressive because they are getting their anger out; it is passive because anger is revealed in very "crooked" ways. Rather than telling you what upsets them, they are likely to choose an indirect means. Often the indirectness is worse than if they were up front about their anger. We have found that this type of behavior is long-standing in passive-aggressive individuals.

The following sample of comments we heard during our study relates to passive aggression:

- "Instead of going directly to the person, goes behind your back to others in authority (usually the others' supervisor)."
- "Passive/aggressive, condescending, martyrdom behavior."
- "The individual was extraordinarily difficult to pin down to a decision. He would reverse decisions he made, literally the next day, and claim no knowledge of the initial conversation and decision."

- "Very friendly, engaging, agreeable, and collaborative one-on-one but then simply doesn't do what is instructed or may do the opposite of what she committed to do."

Toxic People Often Distrust Others. The other behaviors in this category aren't as obviously connected to passive hostility as passive-aggressive behaviors themselves. The common thread that holds these behaviors together is the passive manner in which toxic persons are consistently and predictably able to sabotage any change that isn't directly related to their needs. Distrusting others' opinions in a work environment of teaming and collaboration is a passive way to stop work from moving forward and keeping a group focused on solving the problem of the toxic person. All energy is sapped as the team figures out ways to get around the obstacle in the room.

The following quotations from our survey reflect the nature of "distrusting others' behaviors":

- "The distrust of this individual toward others' work and opinions undermined productivity."
- "Beyond just distrusting the opinions of others, she seems to lack the ability to trust other colleagues in general."
- "He distrusted the expertise of every member of the team and made it impossible to move forward on task by second-guessing all decisions."
- "We had to redo things multiple times and prove over and over again the basis for our decision making. People just stopped producing any meaningful work."

Toxic People Stake Out Their Territory. How is territorial behavior connected with passive hostility? After all, just being part of the human species requires that we have some of those biological urges to own, control, and stake out the perimeter of our physical and psychological territory. Territoriality reaches toxicity when it becomes the underlying motivation for most actions. Being territorial is a mechanism for staying in control and feeling powerful at the expense of others. The most common word used to describe incessant territoriality is *micromanaging*. The consequences of obsessive micromanagement are spelled out in a comment from one of our respondents:

> He needs total control over all elements of all work completed within his division. He literally micromanages to the point of rewriting corporate forms and redoing work of not only his direct reports, but of most, if not all, employees within his division. He has a passive-aggressive nature and undermines other people's knowledge and authority. As a whole, his micromanagement and failure to empower or allow others to grow results in people walking in fear of making a mistake, the team feeling intimidated, and people's confidence being destroyed.

Micromanaging and protecting one's territory are about guarding one's own ego and absolute belief in being right above and beyond all others. Of course, if one person is always right, the implication is that other people won't or can't do their jobs. One of our respondents noted:

> This person does not share and wants to control all situations. She is one of the most difficult people that I have ever worked with; she shames, blames, and micromanages all aspects of the work. Only she can be right! She needs to be involved in everything. She belittles the team, undermines their achievements, points out all errors, and prevents others from learning and being accountable for their performance.

Toxic People Reject Negative Feedback. Most managers and leaders, when confronted with habitual counterproductive behaviors, decide to offer feedback with the hope that it will create change. Certainly they hope that the person will see some validity in the feedback, albeit negative. But this is not so with the toxic situation. One of the most frustrating aspects of managing the situation is the difficulty the toxic person has in accepting negative feedback. The leader is confronted with strong resistance to hearing anything negative, the denial of any and all reports of "misbehavior," and the absolute refusal to take any responsibility in the matter. Consider this comment:

> Even when examples are brought to the attention of this individual, there is lack of choosing to be self-aware and lack of ability to accept responsibility. He doesn't accept any constructive feedback about his behavior. He is always right!
>
> He is a classic "dry drunk"—he rejects or rationalizes negative feedback, deflects accountability, projects own issues on others.

One of the most frustrating aspects of managing the situation is the difficulty the toxic person has in accepting negative feedback.

It is this unwillingness to be accountable for one's own behavior and change that makes coaching alone an impotent strategy to guide change with the toxic person (even though coaching is often prescribed by many consultants and HR professionals).

Toxic People Often Don't See Themselves as Toxic. The last of the characteristics in the passive hostility group is cluelessness about being toxic. How do you give feedback to someone about his behavior when he doesn't perceive he is engaging in the behavior? Yet it is often part of the pièce de résistance of passively hostile persons that "being clueless" or "unaware" of their behaviors and their effects on others becomes an excuse for misbehavior, as noted in this comment:

> This toxic person is clueless about their impact on others; when given feedback, turns it around to be the other person's issues. She doesn't recognize what her behavior is or the impact it has on others. When told, she is always surprised. . . . I don't think she is capable of seeing herself as toxic, but she is unapproachable about this and it is difficult to coach her out of this.

And even when passively hostile people are given clear feedback about the destructiveness of their patterns on the team or how disturbing they are for coworkers, they still deny that they would purposely engage in such behavior, or they justify why it is perfectly appropriate. That's the ineffable quality of *passive* hostility: it isn't visible enough that you can immediately point your finger at it and identify it as hostility. It is usually hours or days or sometimes even months afterward that you realize you have been manipulated, undermined, and sabotaged on a daily basis, as one individual in our study revealed:

> This person seems to be this way 90 percent of the time and has no clue that he is toxic. He is the worst of any toxic person I've worked with. He is clueless about his impact. His behavior has caused many great employees to leave the company and he doesn't care—"just hire another" as if people can be purchased off the shelf!

Type 3: Team Sabotage

Toxic persons were reported as masterful in undermining teams. Ask yourself if these behaviors are familiar from your observations of toxicity at work: surveillance of the team, teamwork meddling, and abuse of one's authority to punish. The following comments provide some of the descriptions of team sabotage that we heard from leaders in our study:

- "Collects information that she later uses against people."
- "Undermines the authority of the team leader and other important contributors by not sharing information."
- "Doesn't provide information to others to get the job done accurately or in a timely way, thus deliberately setting people against each other through misinformation."
- "If something does not go her way, she shuts down, even to the point of sabotaging the group."

Toxic People Often Conduct Team Surveillance. What does it mean to practice surveillance on others? After all, is it not appropriate and desirable to know what members of a team are doing, especially if you are in charge? Well, yes and no. Knowing what other members of a team are doing is an important part of accountability; however, at the extreme, it creates an atmosphere of distrust and intrusion.

Surveillance doesn't have to apply to leaders with direct reports. It can also occur with peers and even one's boss. It's about power, which is one aspect of toxicity that can take a good concept (for example, some form of appropriate control) and turn it into something unwieldy, and even disastrous, for the team.

Our respondents provided examples of the effects of surveillance on a team:

- "Enlists 'spies' to determine who is making negative comments and then takes them personally."
- "During the time that I worked with this person, at least seven other staff members indicated their distaste for this person because of her behavior. She would monitor others' work to the point of other staff members questioning me on who was the supervisor."
- "She monitored me as her supervisor even to the point of my comings and goings in the parking garage. She would also ask other coworkers to tell other fellow coworkers that they were making mistakes and to stop it, instead of telling me, her supervisor."

Toxic People Often Meddle in the Work of a Team. Teamwork meddling encompasses many behaviors that ultimately derail the team's process and productivity. We noticed that the descriptions of behaviors within this type usually involved some form of sabotage or controlling activities.

Leaders tended not to realize a team was being sabotaged until it was too late to rescue the project. Toxic people engage in a great deal of activity behind the scenes that often goes undiscovered by the team leader until the project has failed or the team members leave. Being the last to know about what is happening to your team is not the path to being an effective leader. Chapter Six offers strategies for rectifying this unenviable position.

In addition, a toxic person is often highly skilled in stopping the team's progress by monopolizing the team process. In any group or team, the success of a project can be equally dependent on the knowledge brought to bear on the problem and the way in which members contribute their expertise and work together. The "how" of working together can be greatly influenced by any one member and particularly people who are focused primarily on their own needs, concerns, and position in the group rather than the task at hand. A toxic person can destroy an effective team and disrupt a healthy group process. The following comment points out the results of ineffective and time-consuming interventions on work, product, and team attrition:

> It took a lot of management time to change the group's process, and it produced few results. It severely affected the entire team's ability to turn out quality work with the bottleneck of a toxic supervisor. People left the department to get away from this person.

Some of these specific tactics of sabotage may be only too familiar to you. Over time, groups are immobilized by the constant attention that the toxic person needs daily. The project falls further and further behind, and the team itself ends up with a reputation of being unproductive or a team to avoid. The toxic person is only too happy to contribute to this reputation by going to those outside the team and bad-mouthing peer leaders and staff performance. The cycle of behind-the-scenes sabotage and disruption of the team's process goes hand in hand in keeping things "stirred up" and teams unproductive. In fact in our survey, a label that appeared regularly for the team saboteur was pot stirrer.

In our survey a label that appeared regularly for the team saboteur was pot stirrer.

Toxic People Often Abuse Authority. What are the team dynamics when the toxic person is the team leader? One of the most prominent findings of our study is the use of the power vested in one's position to punish others or demand their allegiance. Bullying others on the team to take a leader's side or ostracizing members who do not support the toxic person's ideas are typical behaviors of dominance, meaning the toxic person wants to control others' behaviors to support his goals.

Many times teams are supported in their work to showcase the leadership abilities of the toxic person, who may take all the credit for the work that others have done. To disempower perceived threats to their authority, toxic people may play the "gotcha" game. And to destabilize any alliances within the group, often those who are preparing to confront the misbehavior or report him or her up the line, the toxic person may discredit those members to peers:

> She does "run-arounds" to manipulate politics and lines of authority. She definitely tries to turn others against them so that she can get her own way. She claims that if you are not on her "side" you are against her.

At times, the toxic person may engage in what we refer to as *intergroup warfare* in an effort to elevate his or her position of authority among leaders who are peers. Creating an atmosphere of unquestioned authority within the team while fostering conflicts across teams, the toxic team leader is able to command the power authority of a leader among peers. Here is how one toxic person consolidated his group power:

> He tolerated and even created conflicts of interest between different projects; he was secretive and devious with those he viewed as outside his circle, but highly loyal to those who accepted his leadership and were inside his circle.

How These Behaviors Work Together to Keep Toxicity in Place

You have probably noticed how many of these behaviors work together to provide an excellent shield for the toxic person to avoid being recognized and made accountable. Toxic people engage in numerous tactics to keep leaders and peers off balance or "off the scent." All of the behaviors we have described in the three types of toxicity contribute effectively to an overall sense of powerlessness in the system. Soon the system has adjusted to accommodating not only misbehavior but also flagrant disregard of company goals and values. It doesn't seem possible that we as individuals and groups would put up with this person and not do anything about changing it. Unfortunately, and at great human and financial cost, we tend to accept these misbehaviors, and often for a very long time,

We want to debunk the prevalent myth that most people will not put up with toxic individuals. In fact, people *will*, and they'll do so for a very long time. Over and over again, our respondents reported that many months, and more often years, would go by without anyone confronting or firing the toxic person. (Chapter Eight offers insight into eight additional myths about toxic people.)

Myth: Most people will not put up with toxic individuals.

In fact, people *will* put up with toxic individuals, and they'll do so for a very long time.

Why does this happen? It is the synergy of several factors in the organizational system working together to hold everything in place, regardless of how destructive it may be. This desire for stability in a system is called *homeostasis*. Like most families, groups, and organizations, many people strive to keep things the same rather than engaging in change. Anyone who has led a change effort in an organization understands the experience of inertia, of maintaining the status quo. The chapters in Part Two of this book cover in detail how to create change in systems of toxicity, but for now, we want to reveal how the toxic person can create homeostasis that feeds toxicity and immobilizes those who want change.

Because there are legal consequences for harassment and abuse in the workplace, these behaviors are more likely to be addressed once they meet the legal criteria. However, there are aggressive (both passive and direct) behaviors that do not meet this threshold and yet have considerable consequences. Three conditions likely facilitate the destructive path of the toxic person:

- His or her relationship with the leader
- The leader's recognition of the power due to position or expertise he or she has
- The leader's recognition of the productivity of the toxic individual

First, the toxic person may have a protector based on a special relationship of power and connection (as we discuss in great detail in Chapter Six). However, you can see from the next set of quotes how this relationship protector fuels the flames of toxicity and allows the problem to continue:

> This individual was someone I worked with at another organization. She has since been "retired" from her position, much to the glee of the remaining coworkers. It seemed the leadership felt they were trapped for too many years because she did cater to the CEO, who protected her.

> This toxic person still remains. They have some protectors in the organization and have managed to get the "truth tellers" eliminated.

Second, the toxic person is seen as critical to the knowledge base of the organization.

> This person is highly competitive, skilled, and has critical knowledge. She uses that to manipulate, intimidate, bully. She really is someone who cannot be reasoned with or who most others cannot work with.

And, third, the toxic person is often considered highly productive and skilled.

> Multiple people within his own division and throughout the corporation have the same negative experience. Most give in or ask for external help in how to deal with him. Because of his division's success, help is often not forthcoming. Some of us continue to push back on him, though we pick our battles more carefully. Turnover has been frequent and high with his direct reports. Unfortunately, his boss protects him because his division continues to grow and make money, although at a decreasing margin.

Why toxic behaviors persist: the toxic person may have any of three types of protectors: special relationship, expertise, or productivity.

Each of these conditions provides a base of power to the toxicity that creates a sense of powerlessness for those involved. Often the leader or peer does not see a way around the protector or a way to challenge the pervasive acceptance that toxicity be excused in the face of a relationship, expertise, or productivity. Are there not highly valuable, productive, and even brilliant people who are truly enjoyable? Of course. But it is time to break the myth that toxic individuals are always critical to the organization's success. They would like you to think that they hold the key to the vault, but in fact, more than half of our respondents reported that the toxic people they had encountered were not more productive than others. Even those who described them as skilled reported that in the long run, they caused so much individual angst and turmoil in the team that they were counterproductive.

The Two Faces of Toxic People: Dr. Jekyll and Mr. Hyde

Some toxic people are chameleons. This is particularly apparent in passive aggression. These toxic people are skilled at knowing whom they can use and abuse and whom they must flatter and cajole:

> This person manipulated those above him very well. His boss was blindly supportive even in the face of feedback to the contrary for all of those that worked beneath him [the toxic person].

Generally those above them in the hierarchy meet Dr. Jekyll, and peers and underlings must cope with Mr. Hyde. You can see how this duplicity prevents leaders from seeing or even understanding what might be problematic in their work group or team. Anyone who mentions "difficulty" with Mr. Hyde may be labeled a complainer or worse. Because those above have no similar experience, they see Dr. Jekyll as a model employee.

The consequences of the toxic person's ruse are devastating to team productivity because the only solution left for many members is to leave. And as the market dictates, it is the best and the brightest who can, and do, leave:

> She [the toxic person] focused significant energy on understanding our organization's hierarchy and who had power. She continually made sure executives knew of her accomplishments. She was skilled at flattering senior executives who appeared to be largely unaware of her destructive effects on those who reported to her. I observed that our information technology senior staff seemed particularly vulnerable to this dynamic. Over the last two years, more than ten people have fled from this leader, mostly by leaving the company. A couple have fled to other internal opportunities. Those who choose to stay live in desperate hope that one of the company interventions will somehow produce positive results. Her colleagues avoid her, exclude her from everything they can except for when they must involve her.

Some toxic people are chameleons. This is particularly apparent in passive aggression. These toxic people are skilled at knowing whom they can use and abuse and whom they must flatter and cajole.

Toxic Behavior Can Literally Make People Sick

Disbelief is one of the first reactions that we notice when leaders or coworkers are coping with a toxic person. They don't quite believe that a person would deliberately undermine the team or humiliate them among peers. However, as the toxic behavior continues and perhaps escalates, the person dealing with the toxic behavior comes to a crossroads: Should this behavior be challenged, reported, or avoided? All too often, none of these responses is possible, and people internalize the toxicity, working with fear and jeopardizing their own mental and physical health. This happens even when the leader has evaluative responsibility for the toxic person and could fire him or her. Perhaps when the toxic person is a peer, a sense of powerlessness to change the situation is understandable, but why does it occur when one is the boss? The following excerpt describes the pervasive effect a toxic person had on a vice president's health and family life:

> I would just obsess about this stuff because of this toxic person. I would come home, and I would be so angry, and I would just spew forth everything that happened that day and how miserable it was and what she did. I was probably depressed and just angry all the time. And, I went to a psychiatrist and he told me, "Well, you know, you either have to figure out a way to cope with this, or you're going to have to leave for your own health." So that's how it affected me personally. I think of myself as a fairly resilient person, but it really brought me down."

Now compare his reaction to a story told by a leader whose peer was toxic:

> Working with the toxic individual was one of the worst experiences I have had in my life. It took a long time to recover from the abuse I received in the workplace. It was difficult because others witnessed what was happening, but they were scared they might receive the same abuse, so they did not want to get involved. Management was passive about the behavior because this person produced work that was viewed as good.

Each of these leaders was strongly motivated to succeed and work with the system toward organizational success. Each of them ended up ill and demoralized, and they finally left the organizations they worked for to preserve their own sanity. The system in which they worked could not assist them. In many ways, in fact, it colluded with the toxicity to maintain the status quo.

Summing Up: It's the Behavior That Matters

Toxicity can raise its ugly head in the workplace in many ways. It is not reserved to any one group and cannot be identified by color, gender, sexual orientation, or race. It is the behavior that matters—behavior that is consistently difficult, disruptive, and habitual. In this chapter, we described three major types of toxic behaviors that we identified from our survey analysis: shaming, passive hostility, and team sabotage. These descriptions give you the language to talk about your experiences with toxic individuals and help you recognize these behaviors long before you, the team, and your entire organizational system are infected.

Now that you have a better understanding of toxic behaviors, Chapter Three describes some of the reactions to and strategies for dealing with toxic behavior that don't work. Why describe these? Because these are the typical strategies and reactions that people turn to. You need to know what doesn't work so you don't waste your time and energy in trying them.

3

LEADER REACTIONS AND STRATEGIES THAT TYPICALLY DON'T WORK

Why Identify Strategies That Don't Work?

This person did significant damage to individuals and our team. There was such a degradation of performance in the function he heads and to the business. No amount of accommodation to his whims changed the situation. It remained that "everyone else" was the problem, and he continued his reign of terror.

—*Quote from study respondent*

Our survey gave us hundreds of examples of what leaders told us did and didn't work. Why review these here if they *didn't* work? By taking a look at the typical reactions to toxicity, you'll likely realize that your reactions, if similar, are not unique. At this point, it is valuable for you to consider your responses to the items from our national survey related to leader reactions (see Exhibit 3.1) and compare them to our survey group's responses in Appendix B (Tables B.3, B.4, Figure B.2).

What kinds of reactions did the toxic person bring out in you and your team? In comparing your reactions to our sample group, we hope you feel less alone now that you realize that your responses are a natural reaction to dealing with manipulation, passive aggression, and other misbehavior at work. Unfortunately, the natural follow-up strategies to these reactions typically do not work. In this chapter, we review the most frequent responses that leaders had to a toxic person and the strategies that they attempted to "defang" the toxicity. We then discuss the reasons these reactions

---

Exhibit 3.1 National Survey of Toxic Personalities: Leader Reactions to Toxic Behaviors

Please think about the toxic person we asked you to consider in Chapter Two: a toxic individual with whom you are working or with whom you have worked in the past. Thinking about the effect this individual has on you and members of your work team, how likely is it that you will take the following actions, according to the following rating scale?

---

1 = Not at all likely   4 = Likely
2 = Not too likely   5 = Very likely
3 = Somewhat likely   6 = Completely likely

1. Leave the organization	1	2	3	4	5	6
2. Accommodate the toxic person	1	2	3	4	5	6
3. Compromise their standards	1	2	3	4	5	6
4. Reduce interactions with the toxic person	1	2	3	4	5	6
5. Exclude the toxic person from important decisions	1	2	3	4	5	6
6. Take responsibilities away from the toxic person	1	2	3	4	5	6
7. Decrease their motivation	1	2	3	4	5	6

and typical strategies often left the leaders powerless, fueled the flames of the toxic person's fire, and ultimately failed.

How Leaders Typically React to Toxic People

To create the survey items dealing with the most typical leader reactions to a toxic person, we reviewed the themes from our in-depth interviews. We analyzed the survey responses and found

Figure 3.1 Leader Reactions to Toxic Behaviors

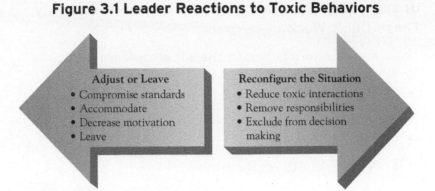

two major types of leader reactions: *adjust or leave* and *reconfigure the situation*, which encompass the seven items in Exhibit 3.1. Figure 3.1 shows how each of the survey items in Exhibit 3.1 relates to these two major types of reactions. Both reactions represent ways that leaders try to manage the toxic situation without confronting or directly addressing the toxic behavior. In some sense, they are passive and enabling approaches.

In case you are wondering if there were different responses based on the type of toxic behaviors (that is, shaming, passive hostility, and team sabotage), the answer is no. The responses are not related to the severity scale of toxicity or the type of toxicity. What did have an influence on responses was the positional relationship of the respondent to the toxic person. Specifically, we found differences in response tactics when the toxic person was the boss of the toxic person versus peer versus a direct report.

There are short- and long-term consequences for leaders, teams, and organizations when they take actions that unwittingly accommodate or enable the toxic person. As we mentioned, there are differential effects given the position of the leader to the toxic person, and we point to these differences throughout this chapter.

Unsuccessful Reaction 1: Adjust or Leave, and Why These Don't Work

These four reactions fall under the adjust-or-leave responses:

- Compromise standards.
- Accommodate the toxic behaviors.
- Decrease motivation.
- Leave the unit or organization.

Each of these reflects the sense of hopelessness and powerlessness that respondents felt in the face of dealing with toxic people on a daily basis. Their own words dramatically illustrate this despair:

> Two months into working for this person, I realized I had made a huge mistake. And I left after six months. When I was working for her, she consumed my every thought and affected my health as well as my home life. Her staff turned over 150 percent during the six months I was there.

Bosses, peers, and direct reports of the toxic person attempt many of these responses to try to cope with the situation. But there are some critical differences in their responses to the toxic person depending on the position the person holds. Specifically, leaders with either a toxic direct report or someone not reporting directly to them but within their span of control are less likely to adjust or leave than if the toxic person is a peer or boss. The underlying factor of this difference is all about power, as shown in Figure 3.2.

When we considered our survey and interview results, we discovered something interesting that explains this difference. With either a direct or indirect reporting structure, bosses perceived they had more control over the situation: they felt they had greater power to do something about the toxic person and situation. With this authority, there was less need to adjust or leave. But less need doesn't mean *no* need: in fact, some of these bosses did adjust or leave even when the toxic person was someone

Figure 3.2 Leader Reactions Based on Positional Power: Adjust or Leave

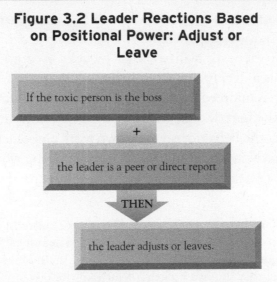

who reported to them—though certainly not to the degree that leaders did when the toxic person was either a peer or the boss.

Leaders reacted to toxic peers or bosses with more despair, having less power to do something about this situation. Those who adjusted or left appeared to compromise their standards more than those less likely to adjust or leave, often experiencing decreased motivation as the only long-term solution.

Clearly, such a condition is highly detrimental to building a stable and healthy workplace and creating a respectful environment. Notice in the next comment that this leader gave up trying to influence the situation when she saw no recourse to provide feedback:

> One of the frustrating things is that as a peer of this individual, I am not asked for 360-degree feedback as part of the normal course. So any conversation I have with their supervisor is perceived as going out of my way to bad-mouth the individual. I tried this once and got bitten; I will not do this again. Instead, I just keep my mouth shut and hope that eventually the negative impact of the toxic personality will become more of a liability to the organization than the person's effectiveness/expertise, and finally someone will have to do something.

When many of us are faced with a difficult personal encounter, our first responses are to cajole the person or accommodate the behavior in hopes it will soon go away. Of course, it doesn't because it is a deeply ingrained behavioral pattern and is essentially being reinforced by these adjust-or-leave responses.

Thus, the very way in which coworkers are trying to reduce the effect of the behavior on their own work emboldens the toxic person to escalate. After all, this person is getting what he or she wants. Here's a familiar example of reinforcing poor behavior:

> One of our clients was a CEO who had temper tantrums. Not just occasionally, but every day. If things didn't go her way, she'd curse you up and down. At one time, she kicked the table so hard, it appeared that she had broken a leg (from the table, not hers!). It was amazing how people accommodated her. They'd figure out the time of the day she might be on her best behavior. There wasn't one. She demonstrated this behavior to those who did not have power over her. For example, no board members or key customers ever saw this behavior. No one appeared to tackle this person—no one, not even HR folks. They accommodated as well.

We discovered from our research that most leaders believe it is often easier to just let the toxic person have his or her way because the retaliation is so awful it is better to just give in, as indicated in this comment: "People are afraid of the toxic person. People avoid her, try to work around her. We avoid contact even when the person's expertise would be of value."

We heard many times that people felt real fear of running into the person or being put on the same team. Others were afraid to speak up because there might be some retribution.

Nevertheless, some leaders confronted the behavior, as did this person, who reported her willingness to go "head-to-head" with her boss over unreasonable demands:

> After one of our yelling matches [with my boss], two of my employees came into my office, literally in tears out of fear that

I would leave the company. I asked them why I seemed to be the only one who had a problem with my boss. They responded simultaneously, "We have the same problems. It's just that you have the backbone we don't to do something about it." So, what seemed like others not having a problem with the toxic person was certainly not the case.

Although yelling is not exactly what we would call a preferable approach, this leader does point out that her coworkers got along because they acquiesced and withdrew rather than confronted. It is a sad lesson for those who want to speak up, because the consequences can be severe. And although this respondent had backbone, her yelling matches changed nothing. Eventually she left the organization feeling depressed, powerless, and angry that no one had backed her up. Peers and leaders alike leave the organization rather than battle the situation alone, as you can see here:

Over the last two years, more than ten people have fled from this leader, mostly by leaving the company. A couple of colleagues have fled to other internal opportunities. Those who chose to stay live in desperate hope that all of the company interventions will somehow produce positive results. It is not just those who work for him who are affected. Even his colleagues avoid him; they exclude him from everything that they can except for when they must involve him.

This exclusion is another example of accommodation. The lesson at this juncture is that although accommodating, avoiding, or confronting might give you some reprieve or at least satisfaction, these types of responses actually have much greater negative consequences to your own and the organization's health in the long run.

Here are some examples of each of these types of responses and the consequences they had for our respondents. The respondent quoted next noted that his coworker turned her accommodation into helping the toxic person and trying to ameliorate the situation; she managed only to exhaust herself with the effort.

The respondent then cited the emotional toll that avoiding the toxicity had:

> Soon I was scared to be in the same room with this person. I began to doubt my own capabilities. I became depressed and lacked the motivation to do the job correctly. Finally, I had to go into individual therapy and take antidepressants and sleep medication to deal with the damage it did to my self-confidence.

And here is a situation that illustrates the power that a toxic person in a position of authority can wield when survival seems to be the only choice for those reporting to him:

> This toxic person is a founder of a multimillion-dollar organization. No one has any power over him. He recruits fawning females for his immediate management team (all but one direct report is female). He's created a cult, and you don't survive if you don't drink the Kool-Aid [that is, if you don't do it his way all the way].

We have concluded that one brave person without a system of support cannot solve the problem of toxicity. After all, if it takes a village to raise a child, then most certainly it takes an organization working together to change the tide of toxicity.

One brave person without a system of support cannot solve the problem of toxicity. After all, if it takes a village to raise a child, then most certainly it takes an organization working together to change the tide of toxicity.

Unsuccessful Reaction 2: Reconfigure the Situation, and Why This Doesn't Work

The three reactions in Figure 3.1 that make up reconfiguring the situation are:

- Reducing interactions with the toxic person

- Taking away their responsibilities
- Excluding them from important decision making

We have many examples of leaders trying to restructure to avoid the negative effects of the toxic person on coworkers. Here is one:

> I believe that this person has had responsibilities taken away from him, but now that he has been in the organization long enough, he is unlikely to have his official position or pay decreased. Even though some leaders have described ignoring his e-mails, others have made it clear they do not invite him to participate in teams, and generally go quite far to work around him.

Reconfiguring tactics are usually open only to a manager or leader—someone with the authority to change the team's or unit's structure or assignments. Our research indicated that leaders who were dealing with toxic individuals who were direct or indirect reports or peers were more likely to reconfigure the situation than if the toxic person is the boss (Figure 3.3). Again, the differential is about power and control, as we indicated with the unsuccessful strategy of adjusting or leaving.

Figure 3.3 Leader Reactions Based on Positional Power: Reconfiguring the Situation

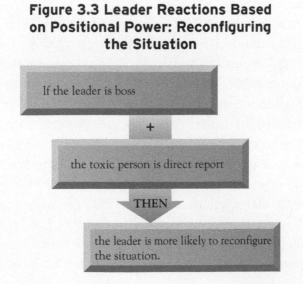

If the leader is boss

+

the toxic person is direct report

THEN

the leader is more likely to reconfigure the situation.

A leader has more power to change a situation with direct or indirect reports and even reconfigure the situation based on power over peers. But this is not the case with a toxic boss. Even with peers, there appears to be more power than with a boss. You have informal peer power in a unit or team and may also try to rearrange assignments to avoid having to work with the toxic person.

However, even when the leader had the authority to make changes in the organizational structure or task assignments, these reconfiguring strategies worked for only the specific unit or team and only briefly. The story one of the leaders told us reflects the amount of effort and time, and ultimately the futility for the organization as a whole, to pass the toxic person from one unit to the next in hopes of "being rid of the problem":

> We had one VP who had two divisions. What they did was they split the divisions into three: engineering. operations, and financial. This left her [the toxic vice president] sitting by herself as head of one division. In this position, she had very little reach. The system of the organization's structure was altered to deal with this toxic person—a drastic but perhaps appropriate action to deal with the devastation that someone of this magnitude can cause. She still sits in a kind of position of authority. And so they're slowly moving her out of that position, and to where I don't know.

Unfortunately, removing responsibilities or excluding the toxic person from decision making does not change the person's behavior, and typically the person simply finds another avenue to exercise her toxic "talents." Likely, we can all probably think of a time when we inherited someone from a different team for no apparent reason, only to discover that the real purpose of the transfer was to get rid of that person. These lateral handoffs are typical of organizations that do not have the authority (often the case in union or government organizations) or bite in their performance management system to recognize as problematic those behaviors that don't reach the threshold of legal action. The types of behaviors that we have identified—especially in the passive hostility and team sabotage areas of toxicity—are difficult to address unless they are specifically identified in performance evaluations.

These lateral handoffs are typical of organizations that do not have the authority (often the case in union or government organizations) or bite in their performance management system to recognize as problematic those behaviors that don't reach the threshold of legal action.

What happens when the situation is reconfigured to remove the toxic person's responsibilities or membership on task teams? Unlike situations where we reconfigure task assignments due to areas of technical or managerial expertise, in this case we are reconfiguring based on the individual's habitual problems when dealing with others. The behavioral problems interfere with the task, and the other working members want the person removed so they can proceed without obstruction.

In this situation, any expertise the person brought to the table is now forfeited by the team. Worse, the behaviors don't stop because they are habitual and well exercised. What has been accomplished is a reorganization that has nothing to do with the project, the deadlines, or areas of competence. It is a reorganization based on personal and interpersonal relations.

Have you ever walked into one of these units and tried to lead it? After scratching your head for the first few weeks trying to find a rational reason for the distribution of tasks and reporting structure, it is revealed cautiously that there was a "real jerk" in the department and they had to organize around him or her. Here's what happens in the long run:

We worked around him by excluding him from meetings, discussions, or simply went elsewhere for the expertise. We also coached others on how to work around him. Some of us told leaders in higher positions what was going on in hopes of getting him removed. These were usually the ones who were quitting anyhow. Some of us started to lose our ability to keep straight thoughts since we were going in 101 directions in a given day. We started to question ourselves and our abilities.

Summing Up Unsuccessful Reactions

It appears that the adjust-or-leave types of reactions are the most likely responses open to people with no formal authority over the toxic person. In contrast, the reconfigure-the-situation reactions are more prevalent with people who have some control over the team or unit.

But neither of these types of reactions changes the toxic person's behavior or promotes productivity, and the consequences of simply accommodating, adjusting, or avoiding have enormous effects on the team and organization as a whole. We find it sobering to consider the long-term cultural effects on an organization that ignores, denies, or accommodates not only the toxicity of individuals but the individuals who collude with them, consciously or unconsciously.

Strategies Leaders Use to Deal with Toxic People

Leader strategies are different from leader reactions. Reactions are less focused, less deliberate, and less strategic in planning and execution—a sort of commonsense or survival mechanism at play. In contrast, there are a number of strategies that leaders attempted to make a difference in a toxic situation. At some point, there often comes a realization that something must be done. Avoiding, accommodating, and adjusting—which, again, are reactions—are only spreading the toxic infection.

In our survey, we asked questions to determine how effective the leaders thought their interventions were in stopping the toxic person's behaviors or simply handling the situation that ensued. We clustered these behaviors into groups that were statistically sound and offered some commonsense ways to talk about these different types of strategies. Consider the items from our survey that relate to leader strategies, shown in Exhibit 3.2, and compare them to our leaders' responses in Appendix B (Tables B.5, B.6, Figure B.3).

Exhibit 3.2 National Survey of Toxic Personalities: Leader Strategies

Please think about the toxic person we asked you to consider in the previous chapter: a toxic individual with whom you are now working or with whom you have worked in the past. Now think about the strategies listed below that you or others in your organization used in handling the toxic person and rate how effective they were.

---

1 = Not at all effective   4 = Effective
2 = Not too effective   5 = Very effective
3 = Somewhat effective   6 = Completely effective

1. Communicating clear standards to   1   2   3   4   5   6
   the toxic person
2. Talking with the person regarding   1   2   3   4   5   6
   the negative behavior
3. Discussing with the person how his   1   2   3   4   5   6
   or her career may be affected by his
   or her behavior
4. Avoiding confrontation with the   1   2   3   4   5   6
   toxic person
5. Communicating with the person   1   2   3   4   5   6
   how his or her behavior violates
   organization values
6. Sticking to my own agenda in spite of   1   2   3   4   5   6
   the toxic person's particular agenda
7. Engaging in damage control by   1   2   3   4   5   6
   cleaning up after them for messes
   they have created in the work lives
   of others

8. Consulting with someone who has a   1   2   3   4   5   6
high degree of integrity within my
organization on how to deal with the
individual

9. Bringing in an external consultant   1   2   3   4   5   6

10. Documenting and then working to   1   2   3   4   5   6
get the person fired

11. Bringing in a team of professionals   1   2   3   4   5   6
(for example, human resources,
legal) to confront the individual

12. Giving the person performance   1   2   3   4   5   6
feedback

13. Managing the negative impact of the   1   2   3   4   5   6
person on my own work

We identified three main types of leader strategies: feedback strategies, informal strategies, and formal strategies. Figure 3.4 shows these types of strategies.

The effectiveness of each strategy was dependent upon the leader's positional power with the toxic person, just as we found with leaders' reactions to the toxic person. We'll discuss these power differences as they are relevant to each of the strategies.

Figure 3.4 Leader Strategies

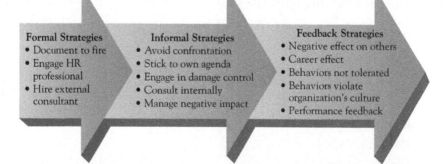

Formal Strategies
- Document to fire
- Engage HR professional
- Hire external consultant

Informal Strategies
- Avoid confrontation
- Stick to own agenda
- Engage in damage control
- Consult internally
- Manage negative impact

Feedback Strategies
- Negative effect on others
- Career effect
- Behaviors not tolerated
- Behaviors violate organization's culture
- Performance feedback

Why Feedback Strategies Don't Often Change Toxic Behavior

One of the most common approaches when the toxic person was the direct report of the leader was to give feedback on the destructive behavior, using one of these approaches:

- Sharing the negative effect the person has on others
- Demonstrating the negative effect such behavior is having on his or her career
- Identifying behaviors that will not be tolerated
- Showing how behaviors violate the organization's culture
- Providing performance feedback

The leaders in our study had good intentions: they believed that if the toxic person knew how he or she was affecting others, the person would surely want to change. Although it turns out that feedback strategies can be somewhat effective for those with formal authority over the toxic person, these strategies are less effective with peers and mostly ineffective when the toxic person is the boss (see Figure 3.5). We have one caveat to these findings: males in positions of authority found the feedback approach more effective than females in authority did.

Although feedback strategies can be somewhat effective for those who have formal authority over the toxic person, these strategies are less effective with peers and mostly ineffective when the toxic person is the boss.

Complicating the leader's own assessment of the effectiveness of the feedback strategy is the toxic person's chameleon-like ability to be appropriate when it serves his or her self-interests of retention or promotion, yet continue to use the habitual patterns

Figure 3.5 Impact of Positional Power on Effectiveness of Feedback Strategies

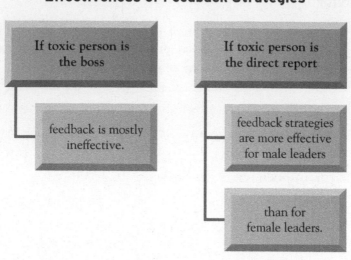

of destructiveness with anyone who doesn't serve that cause. Why was feedback only somewhat effective? In Chapter Two, we related a constellation of characteristics suggesting that feedback to a toxic person has a low probability of success. A toxic person's lack of awareness of his or her own toxicity and resistance to negative feedback make it particularly difficult for a leader to get through to this person in spite of the leader's position of authority.

Peers of toxic individuals reported minimal success in using feedback strategies. They might have tried to give helpful suggestions as a colleague to the toxic person but quickly realized that such suggestions could be easily turned against them. What would start as a friendly gesture ended up a nightmare as the toxic person used the coworker's "compassion" to his or her own ends:

I worked with this individual during my first three years of employment trying to help her with her problems. By year three, I had relinquished my own office in her favor in hopes to improve our rapport, but to no avail. I almost QUIT my job!

When the toxic person was the boss, the only way to give feedback was to frame it as being in the boss's self-interest. Consider this poignant story of a leader who related an incident from early in his career. He felt that his boss had a lot to offer in skills and wisdom and very much wanted his leadership and mentoring in the department. He often tried diplomatically to give his boss suggestions about how he could improve his standing among the staff or how he might give feedback. He called it "coaching up." It was a relatively thankless task, and for all his diplomacy and good intentions, he ended up leaving the company within eighteen months:

> I think the optimal situation is when you have a real sound relationship with your boss and you can have candid discussions about your work and where your competencies and capabilities are. I take that coaching to heart. But I don't get that from this manager, and so I kind of "coach up" and say, "Well, before you tell me what we should lay out, let me tell you what I am doing so far, and then maybe you can give me some further direction."

> It is one of the frustrating areas of the work because there is a total lack of personal investment in terms of helping me in my career. He is driven to look only at the bottom line, and if it's not there, he just tells you to go out and make it happen. He has no interest in coaching down.

Why Informal Strategies Don't Change Toxic Behavior

When it came to figuring out how not to be part of the collateral damage occurring around them, our leaders—regardless of whether the toxic person was a peer, a direct report, or a boss—tried several informal strategies:

- They avoided confrontation.
- They stuck to their own agenda.
- They engaged in damage control with the team.
- They consulted with a trusted colleague who was outside the immediate situation.
- They manage negative impact.

In the short run, these strategies were only somewhat effective. To see why they didn't work better, let's look at a few real-world examples.

Example 1: Sticking to One's Agenda. This story from one of our respondents shows how he managed to "stick to his own agenda" and "confide in a trusted colleague," all while running interference for the team:

> The company had traditionally always promoted people from within the factory, and hiring me was the first time they ever interviewed or talked to a professional trainer. But the manager of the unit was not happy about my hire, and he made it clear in lots of different ways. The more overt ways were coming through my department twice a day—and I mean like clockwork. He would go directly to all my direct reports and tell them what he wanted them to be doing that day. He never spoke to me once. It wasn't like he was doing it behind my back; he'd do it right in front of me. When he introduced me to people, he was always very sarcastic saying, "Oh, well, here's our fancy trainer we got." He'd take these kind of really real subtle potshots and was never supportive. This went on for four months.
>
> My team did what he told them. He was the vice president. It's not like they had a lot of choice. And I didn't have much choice either. So finally I adopted his agenda without abandoning my own. The team worked on both. He paid no attention to what I was doing, but he backed off some when his goals were being met. In this case, our goals weren't working at odds with each other, but the team had to work doubly hard, and we were all burned out in spite of our ultimate success.

In this situation, the leader had been newly hired and was trying to fulfill the goals of his contract. However, it soon became apparent that the vice president of the organization was not on board with bringing in a staff training professional and preferred to train in the usual way. Rather than dealing directly with the new trainer, this vice president chose to belittle him and undermine the team to interfere with the new trainer's success.

This situation is not atypical of the many toxic situations we heard about. However, the leader's strategy warrants analysis. First, he was dealing with someone who was much higher than he was in the organization. And, second, he was new in the organization. Although he was "responsibly doing his job," the power differential and lack of a track record in the organization put him at a significant disadvantage in confronting or directly trying to change the vice president's behavior toward him.

Mitigating these dire circumstances, the trainer did have an ally in the HR professional who had initiated the hire. He often went to this HR professional to vent and figure out how to go forward. In fact, he indicated that without her support, he would have left. Often a strong internal support, someone to confide in, helps weather the storm of toxicity, at least for a while.

The trainer trusted his program sufficiently to believe that his success might overcome the negativity toward him and his team. But to achieve success, he had to fulfill both the vice president's agenda and his own training plan. His team had to meet to contend with the underhandedness of the vice president, the stress that their leader was enduring, and the goals of two very different training approaches. Ultimately the training was successful, but at a cost. Within two years, this trainer had left the company. The toxicity had been curbed with his success, but the cost to the team and to him was too great for him to want to stay.

Example 2: Damage Control. Toxic behaviors have significant and long-lasting effects on team productivity and cohesion. When team leaders become aware of a toxic person's presence and the fallout, they often try to mitigate the effects or protect team members and clients. This excerpt typifies the damage control approach:

> I have captured success by tightly managing these people ... by teaching them how to work successfully with others and teaching others how to successfully work with this toxic person. I believe

these people need to be managed day to day. And at the same time, you do a lot of damage control that can be exhausting.

I also believe it is important to move these people along down the road because the damage they can do to an organization in a short period of time can be huge. It takes much longer to build and only seconds for these toxic people to destroy. Move them along as quickly as you can.

Although this leader was in a position to oversee the toxic person and use strategies to manage him and the damage he created, the solution for her was to move the person out of her unit. It is clearly not an effective solution to the problem: some other area of the organization inherits the problem, and the time and effort to manage the toxic effects resulted in an exhausted leader and a short-lived reprieve.

Why Formal Strategies Don't Change Toxic Behaviors

When the leaders in our study finally decided to use external sources of authority or expertise to deal with the toxic person, it worked best if they were the boss and the toxic person was the direct report (see Figure 3.6). This is quite logical because using the strategies we have discussed assumed that the leaders had

Figure 3.6 Impact of Positional Power on Effectiveness of Formal Strategies

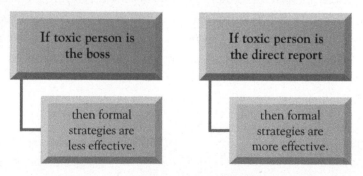

the authority or resources, or both, to implement the following formal strategies:

- They documented behaviors with the intention of firing the toxic person.
- They engaged a human resource professional.
- They brought in an external consultant to fix the situation.

But these strategies did not work all of the time, and the circumstances in which they did work revealed the real story behind success or failure. Our respondents described in their anecdotes hands-on, trial-and-error approaches in which the what, when, why, how, and by whom aspects of the interventions became the critical formula for determining effectiveness. This realization was the beginning of our conceptualization of the systems approach to toxicity in the workplace. Let's look at each type of formal strategy and see why each doesn't work.

Why Firing Doesn't Work. Over and over again, we heard "fire this person" in our open comments section of the survey—in other words, get rid of the trouble as soon as possible. Yet often the leaders did not recognize the trouble before significant collateral damage had been realized, and firing became the last resort after a long process of due diligence.

We counted the number of times that the word *fire* or *terminate* was brought up as the solution in the survey's open comments. The result: ninety-seven times. No other strategy was reported this frequently. However, in spite of the belief that it was the only answer available after what often were years of frustration, this solution did not solve the larger organization damage of habitual counterproductive behaviors that were initiated to tolerate the toxicity but remain after the person has left. In Chapter Six, we discuss in greater detail the strategies for rebuilding and healing teams once the toxic person has left.

Why HR Often Can't Help. There is nothing more logical to someone who has identified a "person problem" than to seek out the assistance from the human resource department. Leaders who manage the toxic person often move on to this step because they have the authority to appraise and terminate. Our findings corroborated this view and confirmed that bosses of toxic individuals were much more likely to seek out the assistance of HR professionals than those who were peers or direct reports. Furthermore, bosses found this strategy somewhat effective overall.

Nevertheless, it was apparent from comments made in the survey that effectiveness was largely dependent on several other factors being in place in the organization. For example, if the performance appraisals did not include criteria related to behavior, this strategy was less effective. Often employees do not understand why their complaints have not been acted on. They are demoralized and disappointed in the ability of HR to make a difference in the very human problems from which they are suffering. To bring significant difficulties to the people who are experts in solving human relations issues and for them not to have the backup from the organization's leadership to make a difference have powerful effects on the morale in the organization.

We are not blaming HR. They often have their hands tied, particularly if there is a protector of the toxic person who is powerful. The organization's commitment to uphold high standards of conduct and protect employees from inappropriate actions from others in the organization regardless of status, prestige, or skill must be visible at every level of the organization. HR departments can be only as effective as the respect and clout they carry to make firm decisions regarding performance management actions, including remedial supervision and termination.

Why External Consultants or Coaches Often Can't Help. Some leaders reported that their teams were in such disarray and the climate so counterproductive as a result of dealing with a toxic member that they sought external support to help solve the situation. However, we found no reported corrective actions that involved external consultants that would address the system as well as the toxic individual. Instead, leaders engaged the services of a coach in hopes of changing the toxic behaviors. But the coaching appeared to have inconsistent results: "After repeated coaching, he wouldn't change, and it seemed that he would only take the situation seriously if upper management took him on." Still another result of coaching was the resignation of the toxic person: "After finally getting her in coaching, she chose to resign in the middle of the process."

These results are not surprising given our findings on characteristics of toxic people and their unwillingness or inability to acknowledge the inappropriateness of their behavior. This makes it unlikely that coaching strategies, focusing on feedback and change, would be easily accepted without a more systemic view of the problem, which we explore in Chapters Five through Seven.

From a positive viewpoint, it could be that the toxic person recognizes that he or she is unhappy and angry as a result of being in the wrong job and simply moves on. In some cases, leaders teamed with a psychologist or mediator to help alleviate the stress of dealing with the toxic person alone. Together, they worked on changing the behavior. Unfortunately, most of these strategies in isolation were only somewhat effective.

However, by combining a set of standard strategies with the help of an external consultant, leaders reported somewhat successful results. For example, one strategy that was somewhat effective was the use of coaching in combination with 360-degree feedback, with an external consultant running the process. The use of a person who was outside the system, with no vested interest in the various personalities and players involved, dramatically helped team members come forward with their concerns and for consultants to deliver objective feedback on problematic behaviors.

Summing Up Formal Strategies

Our respondents described trial-and-error approaches that worked some of the time and only somewhat effectively. The only reports that we received that were deemed effective were taking steps with or without the help of HR to terminate the toxic person. There were no indications that further work was done to help the team recover productivity, morale, or team functioning. After a period of suffering with such toxicity, the initial relief from the stress seduces us to just "want to forget it." And yet groups and organizations, just like families, have a memory that influences their perceptions and actions far into the future. In addition, just like families, a systems approach is the only resolution. It's not easy, but it works. So let's look at the system as a whole by examining organization culture, the subject of Chapter Four.

4

ORGANIZATIONAL CULTURE

How Toxicity Spreads Like an Infection

It was one of those things we discovered over time. Tara [not her
real name] gained a lot of power over thirty years and became fearful of losing
it. She made the organization fearful of what might happen if others didn't
follow what she wanted. In both subtle and not-so-subtle ways, she prevented
people from expressing their opinions openly to both her boss and to people
throughout the organization. Tara alone determined how the structure
of her organization was going to be run, and she didn't want anyone to
challenge it. She found many ways to block people and ways to prevent them
from bringing issues to me because she was the CEO of the organization.

Eventually, even I saw people become fearful of expressing their
true thoughts; they just followed what they thought Tara wanted to hear.
Many were just overtly loyal. The organization finally fired her. And then so
many people came out of the woodwork about the effects of Tara's behavior
on them. We lost a lot of good people because of Tara over thirty years.

—Quote from study respondent

As you may suspect from this quote, an organization's culture
is both affected by and provides clues for dealing with the
toxic person. We recall quite vividly the leader who related this
scenario to us in an interview. He confessed that he was happily
awaiting our call because he wanted to talk about this experience.

He did, and at great length. It was a form of cathartic release, as we found with many of our other interviewees. We were struck with how poignant his recollection was and the remorse he felt for all those good people who had left his organization. If you believe that no intelligent individual would allow this kind of manipulation to continue very long, we'd like to share a bit more about this situation. This was a hospital system with many educated professionals: nurses and physicians of every specialty and subspecialty imaginable, laboratory supervisors, medical and nonmedical executives, and food service managers, to name just a few of the many in the trenches of this soured culture. So how could such a situation occur and for so long? This chapter uncovers some of the reasons that sick cultures persist and recommends approaches for turning them into healthy environments that prevent the spread of a toxic infection.

We also provide the results of our statistical analyses around the organization's culture. Two main factors emerged from our analysis and are summarized in Figure 4.1:

- System dynamics address the ways in which the organization promotes or inhibits toxicity.

Figure 4.1 Organizational Culture: System Dynamics and Organizational Values

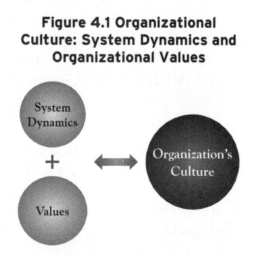

- The organization's values identify the principles or standards an organization uses to deal with respectful engagement, which ultimately affects how an organizational culture deals with toxicity.

We explore each of these in great detail throughout this chapter.

Evaluate Your Organization's Culture

Before we explore in detail the culture that allows toxicity to continue, we invite you to answer a few sample questions extracted from our national survey. These are the items that deal with the organization's culture—in this instance, *your* organization's culture. Just as in our research study where participants had to consider one toxic individual with whom they have dealt, we're asking you to do the same. Answering the questions in Exhibit 4.1 will provide you with a better sense of our study and, more important, an awareness of your own reactions as you reflect on one specific toxic individual with whom you have dealt in the past (or perhaps with whom you are currently dealing).

To understand the meaning of your responses toward the one toxic individual you have identified, there are two statements that are "positive": items 1 and 6. If you scored high on these items (either *agree* or *strongly agree*), your organization is probably in good stead with setting up a proactive culture in dealing with toxic personalities. The remainder of the items are "negative": if you scored high on them (again, either *agree* or *strongly agree*), your organization's culture has a high probability of promoting toxicity.

Turn to Appendix B (Tables B.7, B.8, Figure B.4) to compare your responses to the average percentages we obtained from our sample of four hundred leaders.

Exhibit 4.1 National Survey of Toxic Personalities: Organizational Culture

Please think about the toxic person we asked you to consider in previous chapters: a toxic individual with whom you are working or with whom you have worked in the past. With respect to the following factors associated with the toxic individual's immediate work environment, how strongly do you agree or disagree with these statements?

1 = Strongly disagree   4 = Somewhat agree
2 = Disagree   5 = Agree
3 = Somewhat disagree   6 = Strongly agree

1. Our organizational values provide concrete behaviors in how we deal with the toxic person	1 2 3 4 5 6
2. The climate changes when the toxic person is present	1 2 3 4 5 6
3. The structure of the organization changes to accommodate the toxic person's behaviors	1 2 3 4 5 6
4. It takes a long time for the toxic person's behavior to come to the attention of the leaders in the organization	1 2 3 4 5 6
5. The organizational environment contributed to the toxic person's getting away with counterproductive behaviors	1 2 3 4 5 6
6. Our organizational culture has a low tolerance for toxic behaviors	1 2 3 4 5 6
7. Our organization tolerates toxicity if the person is productive	1 2 3 4 5 6
8. Team meetings are less productive	1 2 3 4 5 6

Our analysis of these items resulted in two distinct categories that make up the organization's culture in relation to toxicity (see Figure 4.1). These two categories—system dynamics and organizational values—and the factors that contribute to their meaning are addressed in the remainder of this chapter.

System Dynamics: How an Organization's Culture Can Promote Toxicity

We discovered six primary ways in which an organization promotes toxicity:

1. The structure changes to accommodate the toxic personality.
2. The organization tolerates the toxicity, provided the individual is productive.
3. The team climate changes when the toxic person is present.
4. The organization's leaders are unaware of the toxic person's behavior.
5. Less productive team meetings are tolerated.
6. The organization contributes to the toxic person getting away with counterproductive behaviors.

Although leaders of the organization may not be intentionally creating an environment that facilitates a toxic person's influence, nonetheless their lack of knowledge about these issues will serve the interests of the toxic person rather than the organization. The findings from our research provided some important insights into how system dynamics emerge and how they reflect organizational values. Let's look at each of these six situations in more detail.

The Structure Changes to Accommodate the Toxic Personality

Think about your own organization or community. Does the structure change based on the needs and wants of the toxic person? To answer this question, consider what we mean by *structure change*. As consultants, if we had a dollar every time a leader came to us to help him or her "restructure" the organization, we'd be millionaires on that statistic alone. Well, not really, but we hope you get the point that restructures are not all they are cracked up to be.

Restructuring is often code for something else (for example, "I don't know how to handle this person, so let's restructure"). It doesn't even have to be related to a toxic personality for restructuring to be requested (for example, "I'm having strategic issues with the team, so let's restructure"). No matter what the reason, restructures don't work very often.

In one study after another, restructures related to mergers and acquisitions alone, for example, work only about 25 percent of the time. And that's the optimistic view. The data indicate that restructures based on a merger and acquisition typically fail to accomplish the goals to which they initially set out anywhere from 70 to 75 percent of the time.

And just as in mergers and acquisitions, we have discovered that restructuring a work unit to accommodate a toxic person has a relatively high probability of being doomed. Examples of restructuring around the toxic person are transferring key work away from the individual, reassigning some tasks so there was less interaction with certain people, and finding a role for the person to make a significant contribution to the organization but removed from client contact and isolated from other staff as much as possible.

Therefore, as consultants, when we are asked whether a client should try a restructure based on the toxic individual, we say no. However, if a client is insistent about at least trying this route, we suggest that it be for a limited period of time. If it isn't working, the leader should give up on this strategy and move on to more productive interventions (which we discuss in Chapters Five through Seven).

The Organization Tolerates Toxicity, Provided the Individual Is Productive

We want to dispel any rumors that toxic people remain in the organization because they are productive: some are productive, but others are not. What we have discovered is that their behavior is more likely to be tolerated when they are productive.

When toxic individuals are productive, there is more of a hands-off approach to them, as this leader commented:

> The organization's tolerance for toxic behaviors is inconsistent.
> I have seen some toxic personalities get fired very quickly; others remain for decades. The key seems to be whether that person has a skill or area of expertise that may be difficult to replace.

As consultants with significant psychological training, we see this as classic enabling. Individuals around the toxic person need to recognize that enabling is not helpful to anyone but the toxic person. Enabling involves a variety of behaviors. Some that we have seen include turning the other cheek during some of the toxic person's bouts of anger in order to keep the peace. Other enabling behaviors entail agreeing with the individual so as not to arouse his or her suspicion that you really don't see the person's point of view because if you disagree, trouble can loom. Essentially, enabling entails any host of behaviors that allow the behavior to continue by your doing nothing or doing something that says to the toxic person that you're on his or her side.

Once leaders recognize that enabling is occurring, they will better understand what's below the tip of the iceberg: the hidden costs of allowing the "productive" individual to continue his or her behaviors and ultimately remain in that job. We place "productive" in quotes because although some toxic people may appear to be productive on the surface, the intensity of their successes is reduced by the many hidden costs of their "productivity": others leaving the organization, not wanting to work with them, polarizing staff, or engaging in a host of passive-aggressive behaviors that do serious harm to both the team and the organization. But even though these detrimental behaviors occur, they are sometimes overlooked in the guise of productivity. Here's what some of our respondents have said about this issue:

- "It is very difficult to deal with toxic people when they are good producers. They seem to get away with treating others badly because they produce results."
- "Staff within the area recognize the individual's level of commitment and passion toward patient care; they continue to tolerate and look beyond the toxic behaviors."

And then there are toxic people who are not productive. Why do they continue? We have heard many different rationales for retaining the toxic person through our research and our own consulting practices:

- It's too draining to deal with the toxic individuals.
- It's "impossible" to get rid of them.
- It's just plain easier for others to leave the organization.
- Many just don't know how to tackle them when the toxic person is gifted at debating.

Do any of these rationales ring true for you?

The Team Climate Changes When the Toxic Person Is Present

A substantial majority—87 percent—of our survey respondents either "agreed" or "strongly agreed" that the climate changes when the toxic person is present. And an alarming 99 percent of the responses ranged from "somewhat agreed" to "strongly agreed." The following quotes from some of our respondents illustrate what these changes might entail:

- "He was in a position of authority, so his mediocrity and passive-aggressive behavior were like poison for the team over time. People got angry behind his back, covered for him, and even ignored him, which did not promote the team working at its best."
- "The entire team walked on eggshells in front of her."
- "He created a lack of trust that has undermined the goals of the department and the organization."
- "People choose not to attend meetings when she is present."
- "Incredibly low team morale is a top concern as a result of this toxic person."
- "The toxic person creates an us-versus-them among the individual's team and other teams."
- "Her behavior was so extreme that people were almost immobilized."

As you can see from these quotes, the people around the toxic person are negatively affected by their toxicity. This manifests itself in such climate changes as a reduction in the team's morale demonstrated by team members being less willing to contribute to meaningful discussions, less likely to volunteer for challenging assignments, and even less prone to challenge each other for fear of arousing the ire of the toxic individual.

A substantial majority—87 percent—of our survey respondents either "agreed" or "strongly agreed" that the climate changes when the toxic person is present.

A serious manifestation that many leaders do not consider is the impact the climate change has on the organization's or community's customer or client base. Toxicity spreads not just within the immediate environment but to other departments, communities, customers, and clients. As consultants, we have heard about such "epidemics." During these times, it is amazing to learn what customers have heard and know about the organization, including the profound effects of the toxic person. If only a leader (and others) realized what was being said about their organization or community.

Toxicity spreads not just within the immediate environment but to other departments, communities, customers, and clients.

The Organization's Leaders Are Unaware of the Toxic Person's Behavior

It often takes a long time for the toxic person's behavior to come to the attention of the leaders of the organization. What goes on in the culture of an organization that produces this kind of response? Why is the leader sometimes the last to know? The data from our interviews and our surveys appear to be a result of two key factors: enabling behaviors and dimensions of power.

How Leaders Enable Toxic People. Let's look at enabling here in a slightly different slant from the ones we presented in the previous section. In this context, the leader is helping the toxic person continue her productivity path. Although it may appear that it takes a long time to garner the attention of leaders, what we have discovered in our consulting practices is that in some contexts, leaders do know what's going on. And the reason they allow the toxic behavior to continue is one we provided earlier: the leader perceives the toxic person as bringing something of value to the organization, that is, this person is "productive." Subsequently the leader may pull out all the stops, run interference for the toxic individual, and provide stepping-stones to help him or her be even more productive, all while he or she continues his or her path of mass destruction. This is enabling at its finest.

The leader may pull out all the stops, run interference for the toxic individual, and provide stepping-stones to help him or her be even more productive.

Some Leaders Aren't Open to Hearing About Toxic Behavior. The second issue—the dimension of power—is strongly related to the fact that some leaders are not open to feedback. In the executive consulting we have done, there is often one issue that leaders have voiced to us repeatedly: "Why aren't people more honest with me? Why won't they give me feedback on what's really going on in the organization?" These questions indicate a paradox.

First, some leaders really don't want people to be truly honest with them. Some don't want feedback even though they say they do. Perhaps one reason they invite feedback is their understanding that good leaders *should* solicit feedback. Dealing with toxic personalities is messy, so sometimes leaders perceive it's much easier to leave the issue alone than to try to tackle the toxic individual.

Second, there is no system of values in place to help them have a context for dealing with toxic individuals. We'll explore precisely how to engage the organization in designing values in Chapter Five. Values may also not be effectively communicated throughout the organization, or there may not be a performance management system in place that ties these values to the kind of culture expected in the organization.

Third, the toxic person may indeed be productive. In this situation, some leaders are reluctant to rock the boat, even though they see high turnover, reduced team motivation, and increased costs of recruiting, to name just a few negative impacts on the rest of the organization.

Finally, the big question is how long toxicity takes to come to the attention of leaders. There are obviously varied answers, but some of the more telling remarks in our survey included these:

- "It took almost two and a half years and immeasurable costs."
- "We lost a lot of good people over thirty years because of Tara."

And even when a leader knows that there is toxicity in the organization, the behaviors may be so ingrained in the culture that people become habituated to them and begin to believe that is just the way things are normally. Also contributing to the longevity of the problem is that new victims come and go, sometimes because of the toxic individual. Toxic behaviors become the status quo, allowing them to dominate the organizational culture through an unintentional but lethal process.

Less Productive Team Meetings Are Tolerated

Toxic individuals have a tendency to promote mediocrity in their teams, even though a toxic person may be more productive than the others. The research we related in Chapter One is that the lowest team member's score on such items as agreeableness and emotional stability was a better predictor of team success than either the team's overall mean personality score or the highest person's score. So if you want to know how a team is doing, look for the team member who exhibits the most emotional instability. Moreover, the lowest member's score for conscientious and agreeableness predicts group performance better than cognitive ability does. Finally, a team made up of two emotionally unstable and two stable members performed as poorly as the group of all unstable members. In other words, one bad apple does spoil the bunch. The toxic person has the potential to reduce the team's culture to one that is demotivating and less productive, as these respondents' descriptions point out:

- "This was someone whom I had mentored, so the deception was even more toxic. I have since had more trouble trusting people in my new workplace environment; it poisons your view of coworkers."

- "It took some time to fix the damage done to the culture. We had to take time and find a very good replacement and then rebuild trust with staff."

- "They tend to pollute the environment with their negativity. I have seen others quit at a previous organization as a result of their behaviors."

- "We found ourselves adopting the toxic person's behavior, and teamwork became nonexistent."

- "Some people actually left after more than twenty-five years with the company when this person wasn't fired."

Organizations Can Enable Toxic Behaviors

In understanding how an organization contributes and actually enables the toxic person to get away with such counterproductive behaviors, it is important to recognize the interactive effect of power differentials between the leader and the toxic person, and systemic factors.

First, in terms of power differentials, our research showed that leaders who have people with toxic personalities reporting to them are less likely to see a systemic problem than if the toxic person is their peer or boss. It's almost as if power is bliss. Leaders of toxic individuals see far less significance than do leaders who don't have toxic people reporting to them of how the system reinforces toxic personalities. In contrast, if the toxic person is your peer or boss, you will likely see the systemic dimensions of the problem much more so than if this toxic person is your direct report. One of the leaders in our study documented this perspective of how less aware leaders are of the systemic effects of toxicity:

> I have captured success of working with toxic personalities by tightly managing these people...by teaching them how to work successfully with others and teaching others how to work successfully with the toxic person. I believe these people need to be day-to-day managed. You need to do a lot of damage control, and this can be exhausting.
>
> I also believe it's important to move these people along down the road because the damage they can do to an organization in a short period of time can be huge.... It takes much longer to build and only seconds for these toxic people to destroy. Move them along as quickly as you can.

This leader never mentions the power of the system concerning toxicity. Moreover, when we examined the data, the type of one-on-one interventions this leader addresses is not corroborated by our research. That is, we did not find that these kinds of typical one-on-one feedback processes work very well in isolation of the entire system perspectives that would certainly include values identification and values alignment with core behaviors. Although perhaps one leader may have success with this feedback approach, it is still not the most effective and efficient way to deal with toxic personalities. Also, please note that this leader does not report success of this one-on-one feedback approach! The bottom line is that you should first implement system approaches, and then work with individual approaches.

The second effect of power differentials that is important to values-based approaches in dealing with toxicity is reporting relationships. Once again, power differentials—whom the leader has direct influence over—affect the success of working with a toxic person.

Leaders with a toxic direct report don't rely on organizational values to deal with toxic personalities as much as do leaders with a toxic peer or boss. Leaders of toxic people appear to be enmeshed in the web that toxic personalities weave. They try managing the toxic person's performance directly through discussions, with incentives, and even with punishment, such as withholding monetary incentives. Although some of these could work, it is far more effective to look beyond the toxic person to the concrete values of the organization. And if the organization doesn't have these in place, leaders should help the organization understand the importance of engaging these perspectives. The reason is that leaders who have toxic persons reporting to them believe that values do exist in the organization that do not tolerate toxicity. In contrast, peers and those who have toxic bosses believe that organizational values do not exist related to toxicity and that their organization tolerates toxic behavior. In Chapters Five through Seven, we focus on how a leader can embrace both of these discrepant perspectives and put a healthy organization in place, as demonstrated by this quote from one of our study participants:

> I would add that the past administration was tolerant of this toxic behavior. This administration addressed it immediately, which has set the bar for what will be acceptable. Naturally, this has allowed an overall health for the entire organization, which has brought in even healthier team members.

How the Organizational Culture Contributes to Toxicity

The second organizational culture dimension relates to the values of the organization. Toxicity flourishes in situations in which the organization does not provide concrete, behaviorally specific values and has a high tolerance for toxic behaviors. Many organizations have stated values, but stating these is not enough when it comes to toxicity. The values we learned about in our research study were those that were so specific, there were few opportunities for misinterpretation *and* they were promoted in the daily work of the organization.

Consider a value that many organizations have in some form: the value of integrity. This tells us very little in guiding human behavior because integrity can mean different things to different people. Instead, think of integrity in relation to respectful relationships with others in the organization. The behaviorally specific terms listed below were developed in a values clarification activity we conducted with a small technology firm. This was part of a two-day strategic planning session in which the group wanted to make sure their values were not only aligned with the mission of the organization but also well specified so that they would become a part of the daily work of every employee. One of the five values they centered on was integrity. Here is what they came up with as a group regarding this one value:

- Not talking behind someone's back
- Providing feedback to someone in the way we would like to receive feedback
- Waiting a period of time before providing someone with negative feedback to be sure that you are delivering the message with both honesty and courtesy
- Taking responsibility for our own actions

Now think through how your team, unit, or organization might define integrity.

Toxicity will be significantly reduced in organizations that clearly define the values in concrete ways, identify the kinds of behaviors the organization will and will not tolerate, and have a clear set of consequences when an individual does not live up to the values. Of course, the leader must model these behaviors as well. Walking the talk is key.

Toxicity will be significantly reduced in organizations that clearly define the values in concrete ways, identify the kinds of behaviors the organization will and will not tolerate, and have a clear set of consequences when an individual does not live up to the values.

Here is what one leader said on how he used these values to weed out toxic personalities. What's even more interesting is that this individual was in the federal government—a domain that many perceive as only rarely terminating someone's employment:

One of the things that's tough to do is lay out strategies and values. And you can't get rid of somebody because they're a sourpuss, but you can get rid of somebody if the strategies they use are unethical. So when I was in government, everybody told me you can't fire anybody. I fired people. . . . And the way you fire them is by first being very clear, very explicit about what your goals are, what the strategies are that you're going to achieve, how you use these to achieve the goals, and the value system you are going to have. If you have these values, if you clearly enunciate them, and hold people accountable to them, then you can get rid of an aberrant personality.

In Chapters Five through Seven on intervention systems, we identify how leaders go about creating a culture with concrete, behaviorally anchored values and demonstrate through action a low tolerance for violation of these values. These values must be clearly identified and articulated so they become a part of every leader's and organization's equation in dealing with behaviors that can detract from an organization's success. These values become the threshold that must be maintained, and there are clear consequences for consistently failing to honor these values.

Leaders have two courses of action in defining values. One is a proactive stance: they create these values through a process of codesign with other key stakeholders. The other is a reactive stance: what they do when someone violates these values. Both situations are explored in the next several chapters, where we identify the systems and leadership changes needed.

Summing Up

Organizational culture is a critical part of the equation in understanding and dealing with toxic personalities. Yet it has been neglected for a long time because many believe that one-on-one approaches with the toxic person were the best solution. In fact, a leader who understands the organization's culture is much better positioned to deal with the toxic personality. It's sort of an economies-of-scale approach: use scarce resources wisely. And by understanding critical cultural dimensions, you'll be using your resources in the most effective ways.

Let's turn to Part Two of the book, which looks at how to change workplace toxicity at the organizational, team, and individual levels. We begin in Chapter Five with the organizational level.

Part Two

The Toxic Organization Change System Model

Leaders have three avenues to address toxicity in organizations:

- The large organization system, covered in Chapter Five
- The smaller team system, described in Chapter Six
- One-on-one interventions directly with the toxic individual, reviewed in Chapter Seven

Before we focus on these three levels, however, we would like to provide you with an overall road map of these avenues for change. Our Toxic Organization Change System (TOCS) model is dynamic and reflects the belief that any change in the system affects all other parts of the system either directly or indirectly. This is commonly known as the butterfly effect, conceptualized by meteorologist Edward Lorenz's discovery in the 1960s that large-scale consequences can be realized in complex systems because of minute initial changes.[1]

Thus, toxic behavior has significant influence on peers, direct reports, and management not only in reference to behavioral reactions, but in terms of productivity, creativity, and retention. These effects were voiced in our study and have been corroborated by other researchers of counterproductive behaviors.[2] The longer the toxic behaviors are tolerated and accommodated, the more widespread the impact.

Our TOCS model takes the position that all parts of the system are vulnerable to toxicity, so effective solutions must be capable of addressing the problem at the system, team, and individual levels. This approach is counterintuitive to how most leaders deal with toxicity because there is a natural gravitation to individual interventions of giving the toxic person feedback or firing the individual. Although these might seem like logical first responses, they often don't work as effectively as leaders would like. Even the ultimate action of termination does not address the debris field left behind after the toxic person has left, and it does not establish organizational policies that will prevent the problem. As we discussed in Chapter One, the amount of time, money, and person power expended in first recognizing that there is a problem can be staggering. Furthermore, the process of termination itself does not address how to reduce the probability that this won't happen again in the future.

Figure II.1 illustrates the primary components that intersect to create a systems view of the problem of toxicity. Notice that the foundational elements of the TOCS model—organizational, team, and individual strategies—are connected.

The strategies used in our model contribute to the development and maintenance of an environment of respectful engagement. It is important to consider all levels of intervention when dealing with toxicity or trying to prevent it. Ideally, an organization is able to set the standards for respectful engagement at the organizational level, thus allowing teams and individual managers to build norms for behavior at their levels. However, it

Figure II.1 Toxic Organization Change System (TOCS)

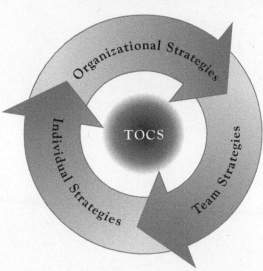

isn't always possible to start with the larger system of the organization, so we propose effective strategies for intervention when starting from any of the three levels of the model: organizational, team, or individual.

5

ORGANIZATIONAL STRATEGIES

Dealing with Toxicity at the Highest System Level

The past administration was tolerant of toxic individuals. This administration addresses it immediately, which has set the bar for what is acceptable. Naturally, this has allowed an overall health for the entire organization, which has brought in even healthier team members.

—Quote from study respondent

We are realists, so we don't expect all leaders to have the power or resources to intervene with the entire organizational system. Rather, leaders must determine what they have the opportunity (and even power) to change.

The leaders we surveyed and interviewed recited the various methods that they had tried to change a toxic person or rescue a team from their effects. It became clear that without system backup, the toxicity would be ignored or transferred to another unit in the organization. In spite of limited effectiveness, the leaders we surveyed and interviewed nevertheless were able to identify what went wrong when they tried various strategies and why they thought the strategies didn't work. By carefully examining their comments, we extracted a set of simple principles that can guide successful interventions with toxic situations:

Principles of the TOCS Model

- Interventions that engage a combination of organizational, team, and one-on-one methods have the highest probability of success.

- If you cannot implement strategies for change at all three levels, start with the organizational first and the team second rather than the one-on-one level.

- The person in the organization who has sufficient organizational authority to enact clear consequences is the one to address the one-on-one strategies with the toxic person.

Although initially it may seem daunting to tackle these changes to deal with a single person, the consequences of ignoring the problem or thinking that firing is the easy answer could be devastating to the organization. The research findings that we presented in Part One dramatically reveal the prolonged and arduous course of firing someone if there is no clear performance appraisal documentation or no strong organizational policy regarding acceptable and appropriate behavior. In addition, policies and acceptable behaviors must be based on clearly identified organizational values. These values will not only help deal with toxicity and the potential "bad" hire, but they will also create an organization that is clear about its regard for human dignity. And that is good for any organization! We will conclude with the interventions associated with the organizational system, focusing on the clearly defined values.

Formally Integrating Values into Your Organizational System

Organizational values have been the subject of numerous conceptualizations on organizational change, development, and conflict. Unfortunately, many lofty statements of organizational values remain esoteric, ignored, and unheeded in the daily operations of organizational life. It is not that the ideals of such values as social consciousness, team productivity, innovation, and customer service are not worthy guiding principles in the planning and execution of organizational operations. Instead, these values are typically not translated into the behaviors, norms, and decisions of the workplace. Or perhaps they have been carefully spelled out in policy documents but are never reinforced, reviewed, or discussed with individuals or teams.

The formal integration of organizational values can fall into five areas:

- Organizational policies
- Performance appraisal
- Leadership development
- 360-degree feedback systems
- Skip-level evaluations

Figure 5.1 shows how these fit into the TOCS model.

Integrating Values into Your Organization's Policies

One formal demonstration of organizational values that we see over and over again occurs in policy manuals. For example, a value that is in most policy manuals is providing an environment

Figure 5.1 TOCS Model Organizational Strategies

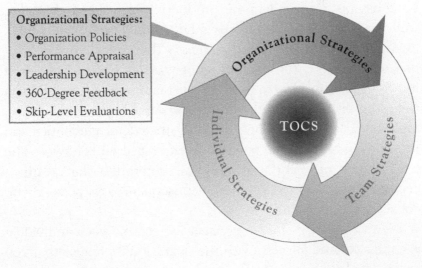

Organizational Strategies:
- Organization Policies
- Performance Appraisal
- Leadership Development
- 360-Degree Feedback
- Skip-Level Evaluations

free of sexual harassment. Most companies have clear policies and procedures around this type of behavior, which is vitally needed and of tremendous support to people within organizations. In the early 1980s, most organizations were just beginning to develop policies of zero tolerance for sexual harassment; you can imagine what organizations would be like today without this policy (and now law).

Values that relate to respectful engagement of each individual in the organization (and outside too, with vendors and customers) have significant implications for creating a toxic-free environment. Policy manuals should incorporate this value and see that it is promulgated throughout the entire organization. The key ingredients for successful implementation of this value are policy formation and modeling of the value by leaders.

Another aspect of the movement toward respectful engagement in organizations is around the sanctions regarding bullying behavior, which have appeared more frequently in policy manuals in the past decade. Some organizations have developed avenues for employees who believe they have been subject to bullying.

The human and financial costs of condoning or ignoring misbehavior in the workplace are enormous. Our research revealed that a large part of this counterproductive behavior—that is, behaviors that undermine productivity, profit, and worker well-being—may not be directly related to harassment as defined by federal law or bullying that meets the typical threshold of personnel action. Yet much of what was described to us in the form of shaming, passive hostility, or team sabotage wore down the motivation and health of coworkers and leaders alike. Thus, organizations cannot simply depend on federal guidelines and legalities in establishing policies about respectful behavior. The leadership of an organization must both determine what are unacceptable behaviors and set out the consequences for persons who consistently engage in them.

We define *respectful engagement* as treating each individual with dignity and fairness, with the operational premise that you treat others in concert with the way you would like to be treated. Dutton proposes that respectful engagement is created by individuals who are genuine, affirmative, listen attentively, and provide support to others.[1] These qualities leave no room for disrespect and incivility.

Organizations that have these core values on critical behaviors spelled out are least likely to have problems with toxicity. However, these values must also be lived in the organization. For example, someone may give a wink of the eye around the value of respect by talking a good game in front of other leaders, but then later, when socializing, say something like, "They want to see respect. I'll show respect when this company shows me the money. Until then, I'm going to run this department the way I want."

All members of the organization must sign on to the values that support respectful behaviors. Leaders must be prepared and reinforced for taking stipulated actions to confront individuals who flagrantly abuse these values. Translating these values into behavioral criteria reminds employees of the importance of living out these values in daily interactions and managing their performance, at least in part, around these values. In Chapter Seven, on individual interventions, we discuss in detail how values can be included in the performance management of an individual with toxic behaviors.

Integrating Values into Your Organization's Performance Appraisal Process

The second area of integrating values into a formal process that is largely unexplored in many organizations is through the formal performance appraisal form. If your organization has a performance appraisal form and has stated values, are these on the form? If so, good! For maximum effectiveness, they must be integrated with the appraisal process. In this way, each person is assessed not only on the core competencies and requirements of their position, but also on how effectively they are working toward achieving the values.

This strategy is one of the simplest to implement. Yet when we ask for a show of hands in our leadership training programs of how many have performance appraisal forms with values integrated within the system, only about 10 percent on average say they do. Human resource professionals (and they usually are the ones responsible for the performance appraisal system) can engage a multidisciplinary team to revise the organization's performance appraisal process to include organizational values.

Integrating Values into Your Organization's Leadership Development Program

The third arena for formal integration of your organization's values is through leadership development programs. Although not all organizations have an in-house leadership development process, many organizations certainly do, and this process is a prime opportunity to reinforce values.

One organization with which we have consulted incorporates a focus on the following items in its espoused values:

- Client centeredness
- Individual respect
- Team collaboration
- Professional excellence

It also has a few other values for which it holds each individual accountable. The organization has behavioral markers that define each value and, more important, carefully weaves these values into its leadership development sessions. For example, when discussing the issues of conflict management, the facilitators ask the group, "How might you negotiate when someone is being disrespectful of you?" And in another session, the discussion hovered around the topic of collaborating in a team "when one person wanted all the glory."

The values alone don't provide adequate answers, and although the organizational descriptors of each of these values help, what was most effective was the dialogue around these values and how the participants in these sessions brought these discussions back to their work teams. These are values lived out through the formal process of leadership development.

Integrating Values into Your Organization's 360-Degree Feedback Systems

Many organizations have 360-degree processes to assess leaders from multiple perspectives: the boss, peers, direct reports, and sometimes key customers. We discuss how to use 360-degree processes in detail in Chapter Six. The point we want to make here is that the most effective 360-degree processes incorporate the values of the organization. Therefore, each leader engaging in this process can receive feedback on his or her effectiveness in realizing the organization's values.

Many organizations use purchased 360-degree systems. Those that design their own system can easily include the organization's values in the process. And for organizations that purchase their 360-degree system, most vendors allow some tweaking in which clients can add items, so we suggest working with a vendor to integrate your core values into this process.

Integrating Values into Your Organization's Skip-Level Evaluations

One of the more robust practices we discovered in our research study was the use of skip-level evaluations, a formal process in which any employee in an organization may either report to, or seek assistance from, his or her boss's boss if the employee is not receiving the kind of leadership he or she believes is warranted. One of us experienced this directly while working for a large Fortune 500 corporation several years ago. Here, the skip-level evaluation was not seen as a way to get back at one's manager or as a panacea for not working with one's immediate boss to resolve the issue, but as a process to ensure that leadership issues would be addressed at the appropriate level of authority. Our study participants reported a similar approach in which they had experienced a high degree of success.

Skip-level evaluation is a formal process in which any employee in an organization may either report to, or seek assistance from, his or her boss's boss if the employee is not receiving the kind of leadership he or she believes is warranted.

Several conditions are needed to increase the probability of the success of a skip-level system:

- A formal policy states that every employee deserves effective leadership.
- Clear guidelines are in place on how to work out difficulties with one's boss.
- Employees are trained in the process of skip-level evaluation.
- The leadership team reinforces the use of skip-level evaluation as part of the performance appraisal.
- Skip-level evaluation is not a panacea to working on persistent team problems.

Having a formal policy for skip-level evaluations is key. Organizations may state the need for this approach differently, but it all boils down to having leadership that lives out the values of mutual respect, is responsive to the needs of employees, and models sound leadership practices. In terms of our work with toxic personalities, skip-level evaluations may be based on the premise that everyone in the organization deserves leadership that promotes respectful engagement. There are two contexts in which this could be applied:

- If someone observes that a leader is not responding to a toxic situation and an employee has attempted talking with this leader, the employee has every right to go to his or her boss's boss.
- If one's own boss is demonstrating toxic behaviors.

In either situation, the employee has two avenues to report the problem: the boss's boss and human resources. This increases the probability that effective action will occur. The skip-level process must also spell out how to approach any difficulties with one's boss before going to one's boss's boss. One of our client organizations has a guideline that is rigidly adhered to: employees may not seek the assistance of their boss's boss until they have at least attempted to discuss the issue with their own boss first. Similarly, leaders will not discuss a complaint with the individual until this "due process" has occurred.

The skip-level process must spell out how to approach any difficulties with one's boss before going to one's boss's boss.

The way employees learn about this process is through formal training and informal discussions within the team. For formal training, it could be included in employee orientation, required brown-bag lunches, and in other existing training programs. It is important that the information be integrated into formal programming. As follow-up to formal programming, individual managers can discuss the process with their teams. We recommend that this type of discussion be more than a one-time

event and is reinforced periodically at team meetings. Nevertheless, some managers in the organization no doubt will fail to deliver
the message, so it is best to have a formal educational component
for skip-level evaluation procedures for all employees to ensure
employee awareness.

Finally, this system is not a panacea. Just like any other
human resource system, it can be abused. However, with clear
guidelines and adherence to established procedures, abuse is less
likely. In fact, we have heard dramatically positive reports about
this process from our own clients, work experiences, and the
participants in our study. Clients have related to us success with
this system when it is a formal process that everyone in the
organization knows about, when it is linked to values-driven
leadership, and when these values are discussed in a number of
different venues.

For example, one of us worked for an organization where an
entire team of employees individually talked with their boss's boss
about a team leader who was disrespectful to the team and created
endless busywork that did not add value to the organization. As
a result of the full investigation that ensued, this boss's boss was
amazed that the situation had been ongoing for two years without
her knowledge. The immediate boss received extensive coaching
but ultimately left the organization on her own accord and found
a position for which she was better suited (and happier, we might
add). The team believed that this positive result would not have
been possible without the skip-level evaluation process. And
participants in our study reported similar results:

> An employee reported to a toxic person, who reported to me, and
> shared with me the toxic behaviors of my direct report. I received
> the feedback from this "indirect report" individually. Instead of
> my simply handling this alone with my toxic direct report, I
> brought the two together to discuss this with me. I gave direct
> feedback, and this person who reported to me understood this.
> She got all teary-eyed, but it was ultimately a useful discussion
> and I think changed her behavior.

Informally Integrating Your Organization's Values Through Leadership Modeling

Although a policy alone is not the critical requirement for successful implementation of values, some organizations place heavy stock in this method for values implementation. Other organizations may not have policies associated with their values, but the values are still alive and integrated into the fabric of what the organization holds dear. They do this through modeling core values of dignity and respect in their day-to-day interactions and decision making. Certainly, not all values are related to toxicity. However, in the organizations that walk their talk, we would guess that at least one-third to one-half of the values have some association with respect for human dignity.

In the organizations that walk their talk regarding values, we would guess that at least one-third to one-half of the values have some association with respect for human dignity.

If the leaders of an organization do not honor and adhere to the highest standards of conduct, then the values are not being lived in the organization. Or if an organization allows individuals who hold key positions of power and authority to abuse the very standards that they are charged with upholding, the values have no meaning. Leaders must embody the behavioral values of their organization as much as they must meet deadlines, improve products and services, and manage people.

In recent years, we have seen numerous national leaders in finance, politics, and religion face the public humiliation and career devastation that resulted from living duplicitous lives in which they didn't model their espoused values. Their fall from grace affected not only the organization but invariably required their families to live through the public embarrassment of their misdeeds and their organizations to take significant losses in reputation and financial standing.

So how do organizations set a standard that they can enforce and imbue in the leadership? Values alignment is not just statements of values and policy; it is the enactment of these values at every level of leadership in the organization.

Leaders must embody the behavioral values of an organization as much as they must meet deadlines, improve products and services, and manage people.

Developing Values Relevant to Your Organization

Large-system strategies in the TOCS model have a core proactive component that addresses the development of organizational values focusing on human respect, dignity, and acceptable behaviors. We discovered in our research that organizations that had concrete, behaviorally specific values and adhered to them had few problems with toxicity. Organizations must integrate these values into their policies, performance management processes, 360-degree feedback systems, and leader development.

However, before any organization can integrate values into existing systems, it needs to *have* these values. We now take a closer look at how leaders develop values and align these with creating a climate of respectful engagement as well as reducing the intensity and frequency of toxicity in organizations.

For values development, we suggest a large-scale process designed to gather feedback from a rich mix of key stakeholders: the individuals who have a stake in the success of your organization. Typically they come from all functional areas in your organization.

Sometimes executives ask us, "Why not just create the values at the top and cascade them throughout the organization?" What we have found is that these kinds of activities are no longer limited to executive suites, and indeed should not be!

We are guessing that some leaders reading this section may be able to relate some horror stories of these kinds of exercises running amok. We have used the model we are proposing and have found it to be extremely reliable and valid.

Involve Key Stakeholders in the Process of Developing Values

There is strong evidence that three outcomes occur when key stakeholders are involved in any change process: greater commitment, a higher sense of ownership, and better results. And values development is a significant change process.

By conducting this large-scale process, all stakeholders have opportunities to discuss, brainstorm, and arrive at consensus on the values that are most important to the organization's success. In addition, they determine the vehicles for integrating these values into existing systems, such as the organization's performance-management process, its 360-degree feedback process (if it has one), and leadership development.

Involving stakeholders in the values process leads to greater commitment, a higher sense of ownership, and better results.

Over the past twenty-five years of working in hundreds of organizations, both for-profit and nonprofit, we have found that the large-scale involvement of others in values creation was doomed to failure when key stakeholders were not included. Their input is critical to success.

Create a Planning-to-Plan Team to Guide the Values-Development Process

Developing values doesn't happen by osmosis once you bring a stakeholder group together. Before any work begins in the development of an organization's values, there is a planning-to-plan (P2P) team chosen by the leadership. This is a small, representative group of leaders, formal and informal, from within the organization: they plan the process of how to go about developing the concrete values. In some organizations, a committee member serves as the team facilitator; other organizations hire an external facilitator. The P2P team is vital to the success of this values-development process because people view it as representative of various constituencies within the organization.

In one hospital system with which we consulted, the P2P team consisted of a nurse manager, a laboratory director, a physician, a clerical supervisor, a union representative, and three vice presidents (of operations, quality, and marketing). This team composition not only provided robustness in designing the values-identification process, but also served to sell the process to others because it was multidisciplinary and multilevel. It is easier to see yourself as part of the process when someone similar to you is there.

The key criterion that becomes part of the agenda for the P2P team is setting out the goals of this process—for example:

- Review the current organizational values, if they exist.
- Develop new values.
- Design a way to integrate values into existing systems, such as:
  - ▲ Our policies and procedures
  - ▲ Our performance management process
  - ▲ Our leadership development program
  - ▲ Our 360-degree system

- Determine if there are potential obstacles to these values in the organization.
- Identify how leadership behaviors support or do not support espoused values.
- Determine which stakeholders to involve in this process:
  - ▲ Just management
  - ▲ All staff
  - ▲ A representative sample of all staff
  - ▲ A specially selected group of staff
  - ▲ Volunteers
- Determine how much time is needed for this process:
  - ▲ A full day
  - ▲ A half day
  - ▲ Two-hour segments over the course of three weeks
- Identify how decisions are to be made:
  - ▲ Leaders decide with input.
  - ▲ Group decides by consensus.
  - ▲ Group decides by voting.

Once the P2P team has completed the design, they determine who will attend the large-group intervention. We have found that organizations usually handpick those who will attend, open it up to volunteers, or randomly select participants.

The room for the group meeting must be large enough to set up several small groups at separate tables. Each small-group table must have a maximum mixture of stakeholders from the entire organization, commonly referred to as "max-mix" groups.[2] For example, each max-mix group may consist of such individuals as an executive, director, manager, union representative, customer service representative, and others as designated by the organization, all designed to represent the broad spectrum of the workforce.

In the values-development event, we facilitate the process by rotating discussions and decisions between the max-mix groups and the entire large group. The final decisions at this session, made by large-group consensus, group voting, or the leadership team, culminate in the final list of key organizational values.

When the P2P process is completed, the team puts together an agenda, including all logistics that need to occur before the values development event, as well as a detailed agenda of how the process will unfold.

The prework logistics addressed by the P2P process begin by determining whether the team or the organization's leaders have identified any special readings for participants to review so they are maximally prepared for this session. The team also designates a recorder for the entire session who will record the results for each activity within the meeting. Then the P2P team sends a memo to all participants as an introduction to why they are conducting this exercise. There could be a variety of reasons, based on the context of each situation. Here are some examples of what some clients of ours have stated:

- Determining why respectful engagement is so critical.
- Living core values is the mark of a world-class team.
- World-class teams refuse to allow others to fail.
- Core values that are truly behaviorally specific and concrete help organizations live out their mission.
- There are three tentative core values that leadership has previously identified that they want feedback on. This inclusive process of feedback and discussion will move these three values from tentative to permanent.
- Everyone will have an opportunity to determine the remaining values (with a maximum of seven).
- These values, based on respectful engagement, will guide our future work.

The team then prepares the agenda for the meeting:

Sample Detailed Agenda for the Values Development Process

8:00 A.M.   Leader introduces the session by sharing the purposes for today:

- Determine the concrete, behaviorally specific values that allow us to become a world-class team through respectful engagement.
- Eliminate self-imposed barriers (for example, administrative versus operational; line versus staff) that inhibit our ability to function as a world-class team.

In addressing these purposes, the leader shares with the entire group her concerns regarding why it's necessary to have respectful engagement in this organization. To help us begin looking at respectful engagement, we'll review our new tentative mission and explain that everyone will have an opportunity shortly to provide feedback on this. Then the P2P team will use this feedback to determine later if revisions are needed. These revisions will be shared with the entire group within the next three weeks.

8:10 A.M.   The facilitator introduces the concept of values planning and the significance of this for respectful engagement throughout the organization.

8:15 A.M.   The leader shares the definition that the P2P team determined for *respectful engagement.* The facilitator invites questions and comments from the large group. The P2P team will respond as appropriate and relevant.

8:45 A.M.	The facilitator introduces some ground rules on decision making as decided by the P2P team.
	Rules of brainstorming and consensus (focusing on support, not necessarily agreement: what you can live with!):

- Cell phones turned off.
- Give everyone a chance to speak.

8:50 A.M.	Over the next twenty minutes, each max-mix group will brainstorm what the core values should be around respectful engagement, considering the three already identified.
9:10 A.M.	Each max-mix group comes to consensus on the top values to realize the mission, including, if appropriate, what the committee has already identified.
9:30 A.M.	Break
9:45 A.M.	Each max-mix group shares its list with the large group.
	The large group arrives at consensus as to their top values that support the new mission. No more than seven core values (including the three previously determined). Less is more!
10:45 A.M.	The max-mix groups break up.
	Individuals volunteer to work in a group, with each group representing one of the seven core values that has been identified. The task for the group is to come to consensus on the behavioral descriptors for the value they are working on. Each group needs to be mindful that the behavioral descriptors should be concrete so that there is little misinterpretation when observing demonstration of each value. In addition, they should consider the new mission.
Noon	Lunch

1:00 P.M.	Each small group shares its result, followed by large-group consensus.
	Discussion follows after each small group has reported.
	The large-group consensus process begins and continues until the final list of behavioral descriptors has been determined for each value.
2:30 P.M.	Break
3:00 P.M.	Each person selects the one core value he or she would like to become a value champion for:

- The value needs to be personally important to the person.

- The value must be one that they can support and contribute to its successful implementation in the organization.

Then each person will receive a personal e-mail correspondence from the P2P team that documents what each person said he or she would contribute.

3:30 P.M.	Each small group shares with the large group a summary of its discussions.
	The large group debriefs:

- What was most surprising to them throughout the day?

- What was most helpful?

- How were they personally challenged?

4:00 P.M.	Thank you from P2P team.
	Adjourn

We caution leaders who are engaging in this process not to form values that are generic. Rather, the values must be concrete and behaviorally specific because their translation into other organizational systems is the foundation to the TOCS model for preventing and stopping toxic behaviors. For example, if respect is one of the values identified, stating that people must give feedback with respect is not behaviorally specific. However, stating that feedback must be truthful, direct, specific, and given to the individual to whom it pertains offers behavioral guidelines that can be observed and followed. In addition, some clients of ours have provided critical examples of respect, for example, not talking behind someone's back, giving feedback the way the sender might like to receive it, and keeping a calm tone of voice when giving feedback.

Make Sure You Can Live with the Values Your Planning Team Proposes

The concern of some leaders regarding this participative approach is, "What if we receive suggestions on the values that I really can't adopt?" There are several approaches to handling this issue. In our work, we have made the following options available to leaders:

- The P2P team determines which decisions are to be made by the leadership, with input from the participants in the actual process. For example, there may be some values that leaders think are critical to the organization. If this is the case, leaders must state this position directly to the P2P team and ultimately to the entire organization.

- There will be decisions that are made in a collaborative fashion. For example, the P2P team may determine that consensus will be the preferred vehicle for decision making: they will seek support of each of the values, not necessarily agreement on them.

- Participation could be viewed as input to leaders, who ultimately decide on the final list of values, with careful consideration of the views presented.

- The decision could be made by voting on each of the proposed values. Although this is an option, there is evidence that voting can polarize a group into "winners" and "losers." Therefore, decision making by voting is a last resort.

The large group's influence on the development of the values will depend on the decision-making vehicle selected. In our experience, the more power that leadership can extend to the entire group in deciding on these values, the more successful the outcome will be.

Summing Up

We hope you now see that the concept of developing values and integrating them into your organization is not a "touchy-feely" process having little organizational impact. This is the prime ingredient that can make or break an organization. Remember the bottom-line results that we described in Chapter One regarding the negative financial ramifications that can occur when toxic individuals flourish in an organization. Add to this the mounting emotional turmoil that can come from an organization without espoused and enacted values. When you link these two components—the financial and human costs—you'll come to truly appreciate the values identification and integration approaches we have presented in this chapter as the foundation for managing toxic behaviors effectively.

In Chapter Six, we move from the foundation of large systemic perspectives to the smaller set of team systemic approaches.

6

TEAM STRATEGIES

Dealing with Toxicity at the Team Level

Effective organizations have to know what's best for the good of the whole team and can't put the interests of one individual above that, or else the organization is going to break down over the long term.

—Quote from study respondent

As management consultants, we are not surprised very often with our clients' reports about either themselves or their organizations. We pride ourselves on remaining relatively neutral to provide our clients with unbiased viewpoints, which are the perspectives they are often seeking from us. This being said, we have to confess that we were very surprised with one particular finding in our research study: we did not expect that one person's toxic behaviors would influence so dramatically the way in which people within the team started to act toward one another. It was not only their reactions to the person who instigated the toxic behavior (which we did expect), but rather that their reactions generalized to other members of the team. In some cases, they picked up the toxic behaviors and used them on each other! In other situations, they withdrew from the team to protect themselves against the toxic person. It was not long before the team climate shifted dramatically, and the team had become a group of individuals trying to survive rather than working toward a common goal. Based on these findings, we realized that teams can unravel when they have to deal with toxic behaviors over long periods, and they need assistance to return to healthy functioning.

A climate permeated by negativity, demotivation, and discouragement does not promote the productivity and innovation that fast-paced organizations need in today's competitive markets. Actions that will prevent toxic climates, and heal them if they cannot be prevented, are central to creating a healthy team environment. Historically, however, these actions have been implemented without a systems perspective in place, to the detriment of the team. What we mean by this is that without implementing the organizational strategies described in Chapter Five, team strategies are less effective.

Does this mean that leaders need to abandon team strategies unless the larger organization deals with the toxicity in the organization? Certainly not. All we are saying is that the probability of success with the team increases with larger organizational support. With this as a proviso, this chapter describes selected team strategies that can either fly solo or build on existing organizational values.

All of these organizational strategies are proactive in our TOCS model because they establish a foundation for the other levels of interventions to build on, but team interventions can be both proactive and reactive. Figure 6.1 offers an overview of the proactive and reactive interventions at the team level; this chapter describes each type in detail.

Proactive Strategies to Deal with Toxicity at the Team Level

As shown in Figure 6.1, there are essentially four strategies you can implement at the team level to prevent and reduce toxicity in your organization:

- Select the right team members in the first place.
- Translate your organizational values to the team level.
- Engage leaders to integrate values within teams.
- Conduct a 360-degree *team* assessment.

Figure 6.1 TOCS Model: Team-Level Strategies

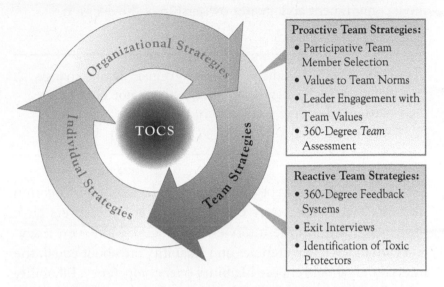

Proactive Team Strategies:
- Participative Team Member Selection
- Values to Team Norms
- Leader Engagement with Team Values
- 360-Degree *Team* Assessment

Reactive Team Strategies:
- 360-Degree Feedback Systems
- Exit Interviews
- Identification of Toxic Protectors

Select the Right Team Members

Selecting new team members is a leader's first call to get the right expertise and personality fit for the organization. It's also the place to avoid hiring a toxic person. One of the most effective selection strategies is to use a participative team member approach.

The team in which the prospective applicant will work can be involved in designing the interview questions and in interviewing. The participation of key stakeholders as early as possible in the hiring procedure will result not only in a much more relevant interviewing process, but will increase colleagues' support for the new person. We regard this as a "three-for-one" win because you increase the probability of hiring the right person, the likelihood of the new person's success, and the intensity of the team's support for the new person.

We underscore the importance of involving people as early as possible. Although it is typical in organizations to involve others in the final stages of interviewing, leaders overlook the power of early involvement in the process. We know from numerous research findings that involvement in any change (including hiring new staff) brings about not only better results but also more commitment and greater ownership of the decision.

Research findings indicate that involvement in any change (including hiring new staff) brings about not only better results but also more commitment and greater ownership of the decision.

We suggest the team be sure to include the too-often-forgotten likability factor (the positive perception the interviewers have of the candidate) in the interviewing process. Moreover, if several candidates' competencies and likability are about equal, the interviewers should choose likability over competency. Likability relates to the development of trust, openness, and connection with other team members, qualities that are essential for good team cohesion and productivity. This does not mean that an organization should hire an incompetent person. Strong research evidence demonstrates that if one candidate has more competence than another but the other candidate is a bit more likable, hire the candidate who has a little less expertise but is more likable. The small difference in expertise can be addressed with good professional development.

Given that several candidates' competencies and likability are about equal, hire the candidate who has a little less expertise but is more likable. The small difference in expertise can be addressed with good professional development.

Even before interviewing begins, the interview questions should be codesigned by the team members and leader. This is a key difference from organizations that claim to have a participative interviewing process: if the questions are not code-signed from the start, team participation is not so strong, the quality of the results weakens, and the probability of hiring a toxic individual increases. This form of interviewing can be done as a collaborative process in which everyone on the team is actively involved with or without the leader present. Alternatively, if it is not feasible to engage everyone at the same time, then staff could certainly submit interview questions individually to the leader, who would then determine the final set of questions. The key to a successful process is to include actual work scenarios rather than hypothetical situations—for example:

- "Please consider an incident from your present or previous employer when you were candid about an error despite the potential risk. What did you do?"
- "How did you handle a situation where the direction for a task was unclear?"
- "In what ways do you think that you contribute to team collaboration?"
- "How have you recently motivated a group of people or an individual to do something he or she was not motivated to do?"
- "How did you provide negative feedback to someone who was resistant to receiving it?"

These questions are quite specific and open-ended, allowing the individual to personalize and add real-world detail to his or her responses. These sorts of questions are important in determining the candidate's willingness to take responsibility for errors, seek assistance from others when needed, collaborate with team members, and change leadership style when motivating others and giving feedback. You'll probably recognize that these sample questions may elicit responses relevant to the characteristics of toxic behaviors reported in our research. We have also discovered that bluffing (and actually lying) is less likely when this model is used.

Interviews should be conducted by the leader and staff at separate times to avoid a hierarchical effect of the leader subtly, or not so subtly, imposing his or her own views or influencing the interaction of the applicant and the staff. Staff interviews should be conducted with different groups of staff as well as individual interviews. With multiple types of staff groupings, the opportunity to experience the candidate in different contexts will improve the likelihood of identifying behaviors that are inconsistent with the organization's working norms and culture.

Whenever feasible, the results of these behaviorally focused interviews should be merged with two kinds of tests: cognitive tests (which measure intellectual ability) and personality tests, with a focus on what psychologists refer to as "the big five":[1]

- Emotional stability
- Extraversion
- Openness to experience
- Agreeableness
- Conscientiousness

We say "whenever feasible" because these psychological tests can be quite expensive, so typically organizations use them only for critical positions. An industrial/organizational psychologist could administer and interpret psychological profiles to determine the likelihood of a candidate's fit with the team and organization. Although this is certainly an expense that some organizations may not be prepared to take on, the drawback of one inappropriately placed individual in a key position could be devastating to an organization, as well as to the team. As we noted in Chapter One, there is strong evidence that turnover costs are about one and a half to two and a half times the salary of the employee who moves on. One of the leaders we interviewed told us, with no uncertainty, what was important in their hiring process:

> Almost all of the effort we put in as an organization is around whether this person will fit. Will they get along? It's less about can they do the job. We can train them to the job. They'll figure the job out. But will they fit? And will they roll up their sleeves and work hard? Will they collaborate? Defer credit to others? Will they put the organizational goal before their own goals? Or is this going to be all about them and all about their career and how fast they can get to the top?
>
> So that's where our energy goes, and most of our interview time and most of the time that we have our psychologists evaluate these candidates as well. It's all about the soft skills.

Translate Organizational Values into Behavioral Team Norms

Without a doubt, the process of identifying and clarifying values is most successful when team leaders are able to depend on the organizational values that uphold a respectful atmosphere. Assuming that the organization has identified concrete and behaviorally specific values, the leader then engages the team in how these apply to their work environments.

We want to note that even when an organization has not yet built these values, leaders can still codesign with the team their own values. We often tell our own clients who appear adamant that nothing can be done until the larger organization has these values that blaming a lack of organizational values on the organization is divisive. Although it certainly would be better to have this organizational support, leaders still can get plenty of positive mileage out of the team's formation of its own values.

Blaming a lack of organizational values on the organization is divisive. Although it certainly would be better to have this organizational support, leaders still can get plenty of positive mileage out of the team's formation of its own values.

These values become a backdrop for translation to the team's unique work setting. When organizational values include explicit descriptions for respect within the organization as well as with clients and customers, then the team can build on this foundation to examine and create ways that the team lives these values. Team building around the value of respect becomes a proactive strategy that helps prevent, or at least reduces, the probability that toxic behaviors will be tolerated and enabled.

To translate the organizational values into team-oriented values, we suggest that the leader plan a team development session. This type of session can last anywhere from one to two hours to a full day. It can be facilitated by the leader, another member of the organization (for example, a human resource professional), or an external consultant.

Organizing this type of team development session has six steps:

Step 1: Explain the purpose of the session with a focus on respectful engagement.

Step 2: Review the organizational values in detail.

Step 3: Set the decision-making process for the session.

Step 4: Translate these values into behavioral norms.

Step 5: Establish a plan for the team to keep these norms alive.

Step 6: Develop a follow-up plan for revisiting how the team norms are working.

Step 1: The Leader Establishes the Purpose of the Session. This can be as simple as stating that it's important that the organization's values are integrated into the fabric of what the team does every day, centered on respectful engagement. Then the leader can encourage others present to share their views on the importance of these values in team activities. In addition, we recommend addressing what can happen when a team member violates an organizational value.

Step 2: The Leader Reviews the Organizational Values in Detail with the Team. At this time, the leader shares a copy of the organizational values. If the organization has done more with these values than just state them (for example, if the values have been integrated into its performance appraisal process), the leader should share these contexts and invite others with knowledge in this arena to share as well. The leader should also invite the team to discuss other ways team members may have applied these values throughout the organization and how they have blended these into their own work. The integration of these values into the fabric of what people do every day is critical to the success of this process.

Step 3: The Leader Relates the Decision-Making Process That Will Be Used. We suggest that the decision-making process be by consensus: all team members, including the leader, support the final list of behavioral norms. They don't necessarily have to agree. In fact, someone could actually disagree but nevertheless agree to support the norms.

Those who say they support the team consensus must agree to follow through on their commitment. Support means not telling others later, for example, that a specific norm is a "bunch of nonsense." If a team member can't support a particular value, the time to speak up is at the team session, not later. This is particularly relevant to toxic individuals, some of whom may be passive-aggressive in nature; they may agree in public and lambaste the decision to others later.

Sometimes leaders relegate the process of values selection to majority rule. We strongly suggest against this because majority rule has a tendency to polarize a group into winners and losers; this is something to try to avoid in these kinds of collaborative discussions. However, if time is of the essence and consensus is difficult, you may have to resort to this less desirable process for the sake of expediency.

Step 4: The Team Translates the Organizational Values into Behavioral Norms. One way we have observed teams doing this is to describe several examples for each value. These examples should be specific and robust, that is, everyone agrees that they see themselves represented in these norms. Some of our clients have translated the value of integrity (often included within the description of respectful engagement) into such norms as not talking behind someone's back, walking your talk, and keeping commitments.

Step 5: The Team Determines How to Keep These Norms Alive. One way of doing this is to provide feedback to each other for demonstrating a specific value or adhering to a constructive team norm. Another is to have "values cards" with a different value on each card. A team member who sees a fellow member demonstrating this value gives the individual the appropriate card with a personal note stating how the person is living out the value by engaging in one of the team's norms. This values-card strategy can get mundane if the values cards are flying around like hotcakes. Nevertheless, when they are distributed judiciously and appropriately, we have seen organizations respond positively to this as a robust way to live out the values.

Another strategy is more formal and one in which the leader takes the initiative. Most organizations have a defined perfor-mance appraisal process, and part of this assessment system can incorporate how effectively each team member has demonstrated the values. This last strategy is one we often see overlooked in organizations. But values are important, and they should be part of everyone's periodic performance evaluation process.

The values should also become part of the informal day-to-day performance management system. In this regard, team members as well as the leader should let people know when they see these values being demonstrated and when they see them being violated. For example, one leader observed someone go out of his way for a peer in a large hospital system, an action that was important to the patient. Another is a leader who noticed a nurse colleague having a difficult time at home and offered to assist that person in finishing up patient care so he could leave work on time. One last example is the leader who helped a peer on a difficult project, and that person's help was the catalyst that got the agency a large community grant to provide health care to homeless persons. In these circumstances, the leader would relate to the individual not only the benefit of what he or she provided but also how it connected with the organizational value and the specific team norm.

At the opposite end of the spectrum, a leader might witness someone chew out a colleague in front of a key customer for being insensitive in dealing with the customer. In this circumstance, it would be important to provide the individual with feedback as to how this violates the organizational value of respect and the team norm of providing negative feedback to others in a respectful way without shaming.

There are two critical points in translating organizational values into team norms. First, it's important that the team members, at the time these values are created, talk through selected scenarios so that they get a sense of what feedback, both positive and negative, entails. These discussions also will help in arriving at consensus because people have come to understand what each value looks like and can make more informed choices as to whether they can support the norm.

Second, it's not just providing feedback that is key to success. It's providing the feedback in the context of the organizational value with the associated behavioral norm. These discussions at the team session are vital to the success of the final outcome.

It's important that the team members, at the time these values are created, talk through selected scenarios so that they get a sense for what feedback, both positive and negative, looks like.

Step 6: Develop a Follow-Up Plan to Revisit How the Team Norms Are Working. Some of our clients have engaged in this in such simple ways as gathering the group together every three months to make sure the team norms are consistent with the agreed-on values and are still relevant to team members. Other clients have sent out a simple, anonymous survey to find out both what is working and what needs improvement. Still other clients have asked colleagues to assess how well the team is working in living out its values through focus groups, individual interviews, or a survey. One innovative client of ours has made this follow-up part of the three-year strategic planning agenda.

A simple follow-up action we have used with some of our clients is the 3C model. We suggest taking just five minutes at a staff meeting periodically in which team members address the following questions related to values enactment:

- What would you like to see *continued*?
- What are the positive *consequences* of this norm being acted on in the team?
- What *could* you do personally to reinforce this norm in the future?

Don't be limited to the follow-up actions we have described here; these are simply examples. We recommend asking the team how best to follow up. You may be amazed at some of the creative solutions they generate. It's all about involvement generating greater commitment and ownership, as well as more successful results.

Developing Team Values Without Clearly Defined Organizational Values

If an organization has not identified a clear set of defined values, then the team must operate without the benefit of organizational guidelines. Nevertheless, the team still needs to consider the larger organizational context. We mean that there cannot be total independence from the organization even though it doesn't have stated values. We have discovered that teams can often cite a few implicit organizational values that appear pronounced and well integrated throughout the organization, even though these have never been formally stated. Either with no organizational values or with informally stated values, the team members can determine their own core values along with associated key behavioral norms.

To illustrate the design of team values around respectful engagement, we have used a model with client organizations without specified organizational values and present it in Exhibit 6.1. It is actually a detailed overview of a values clarification process to identify team values and associated behavioral norms. Here, you'll be introduced to the leader, Jessica, at Navigo company (both fictitious names), and the method we used. In this model, the activities up to 10:00 A.M. relate to the work the team did on its mission. We did not include this in the example, but have included a description of the team's work related to the mission. Since most teams have been through this kind of mission work, we did not include it here. We want you to see how the values work can be attached to other work in the arena of strategic planning, such as mission generation.

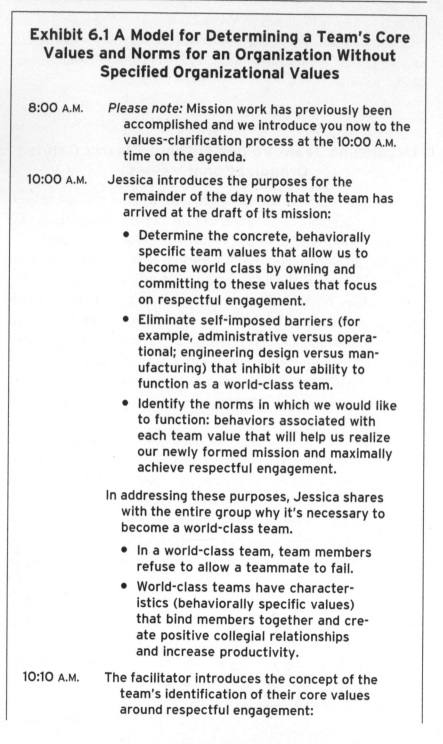

Exhibit 6.1 A Model for Determining a Team's Core Values and Norms for an Organization Without Specified Organizational Values

8:00 A.M.   *Please note:* Mission work has previously been accomplished and we introduce you now to the values-clarification process at the 10:00 A.M. time on the agenda.

10:00 A.M.   Jessica introduces the purposes for the remainder of the day now that the team has arrived at the draft of its mission:

- Determine the concrete, behaviorally specific team values that allow us to become world class by owning and committing to these values that focus on respectful engagement.

- Eliminate self-imposed barriers (for example, administrative versus operational; engineering design versus manufacturing) that inhibit our ability to function as a world-class team.

- Identify the norms in which we would like to function: behaviors associated with each team value that will help us realize our newly formed mission and maximally achieve respectful engagement.

In addressing these purposes, Jessica shares with the entire group why it's necessary to become a world-class team.

- In a world-class team, team members refuse to allow a teammate to fail.

- World-class teams have characteristics (behaviorally specific values) that bind members together and create positive collegial relationships and increase productivity.

10:10 A.M.   The facilitator introduces the concept of the team's identification of their core values around respectful engagement:

- The unsuccessful way many organizations have historically done this, ending in failure:

No "beauty in brevity"
No critical involvement of others
No follow-up

Navigo has chosen a more successful way to plan these core values strategically. You will see this demonstrated today.

10:15 A.M. In max-mix groups, the facilitator will ask members to come to consensus on their feedback of the mission draft. The facilitator begins a discussion of feedback on the new tentative mission statement that has been proposed. The group is reminded that this is input to the steering committee, not de facto changes that will be made to the mission automatically. We are in a consensus mode; the steering committee will be the ultimate determiner of the mission, with consultation from other key stakeholders (for example, executives and board members).

The max-mix group will proceed in the following way:

- Five minutes of brainstorming
- Ten minutes of consensus on their feedback

10:30 A.M. Each max-mix group designates a reporter who reports results of the feedback on the new mission, taking no more than one minute per team. After all the groups have reported, anyone from the audience may ask questions for clarification.

In the large group, the max-mix groups share their thoughts as feedback for the steering committee to consider. The facilitator coordinates the process. The steering committee listens and relates to the group that they will review these items at another time. If there is a revised mission statement that comes out of this process, they will share this with everyone and then seek confirmation from others in the organization (for example, the executive committee).

11:00 A.M.   Each max-mix group will brainstorm what the team's core values should be.

11:15 A.M.   Each max-mix group comes to consensus on its top values needed to realize the mission, including, if appropriate, what the committee has already identified.

LUNCH

1:00 P.M.   Each max-mix group shares its list with the large group.

The large group arrives at consensus as to its top values that support the new mission. There should be no more than a total of five core values; less is more!

2:00 P.M.   The max-mix groups break up. Individuals volunteer to work in a group, each group representing one of the five previously determined team values. The task is for each group to come to consensus on the behavioral descriptors (norms) for each of their values. Each group needs to be mindful that the behavioral norms should be concrete so that there is little misinterpretation if someone is demonstrating these norms or not. In addition, they should consider the new mission.

2:45 P.M.   Each small group shares its results with the large group.

Discussion follows after each small group has reported. The large-group consensus process begins and continues until the final list of behavioral norms has been determined for each value.

3:30 P.M.   Each person shares in the small group the one core value for which he or she would like to become a value champion.

- The value needs to be personally important to the person.
- It should be a value that he or she can support and contribute to its successful implementation in the organization.

Each person receives a personal mail correspondence that documents the small-group discussion.

3:50 P.M.   Each small group shares with the large group a summary of its discussions.

The large group brainstorms the top follow-up actions needed to make these values come alive. After brainstorming for ten minutes, the large group determines where each brainstormed follow-up action would be placed in the matrix (see Figure 6.2).

The reason we are doing this is that we are weeding out the follow-up actions that have low impact. We will first focus our attention on follow-up activities that have a high impact and are easy to implement (quadrant 1). For those that are high impact and difficult to implement (quadrant 2), we will break the follow-up action down into simpler, more manageable chunks.

4:00 P.M.   Closing activity.

- What was most surprising to you throughout the day?
- What was most helpful?

5:00 P.M.   Thank you from Jessica who reaffirms that the most important aspect of the day is linking the values to concrete, behavioral norms around respectful engagement.

ADJOURN

From 10:00 A.M. on, there is a direct focus on the team's values and related behavioral norms. Also, at the end of this exhibit, we refer to an implementation matrix (shown in Figure 6.2) that focuses on two variables: ease of implementation and impact.

Figure 6.2 Matrix for Implementing Change

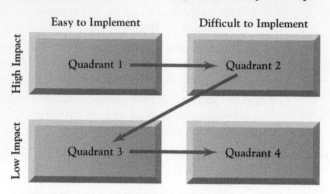

We have found particular success when teams concentrate on the high-impact arena, by first identifying those actions easy to implement (quadrant 1), followed by those more difficult (quadrant 2). Once these are achieved, the team can then proceed to items in the low-impact arena, incorporating those easy to implement (quadrant 3) and those more difficult (quadrant 4). However, we have observed that typically organizations focus just on quadrants 1 and 2—adding more items to these areas as time goes on and never addressing the low-impact items.

Teams can often cite a few implicit organizational values that appear pronounced and well integrated throughout the organization, even though these have never been formally stated.

From this example, we hope you'll see the power of engaging a team in values identification work. Interestingly, the response we received from our client on this process was that the values work would not have been nearly as meaningful without the power of the team.

Finally, although we used this process with a client that did not have identified organizational values, these methods can be adapted to a variety of purposes, including with organizations having well-specified organizational values. The point is that however it is used, engagement is key.

How Leaders Can Engage the Team to Integrate Values: A Case Study

Even the best leader-initiated or consultant-led sessions will ultimately fail if there isn't effective follow-up. Although some follow-up was identified in the previous two scenarios we described, one follow-up action that can't be ignored is what the leader does afterward. That the relationship between leader and the team member is critical has been shown in hosts of research studies. For example, a Gallup Organization research study of performance data from approximately one hundred thousand employees in twenty-five hundred business units found that the relationship with the manager for the most part determines longevity and productivity.[2] And a Watson Wyatt study reported that organizations that communicate effectively were more likely to report lower turnover than industry peers.[3]

Through our in-depth interviews, it became apparent to us that team leaders who kept an open communication path with members about the working environment were in a much better position to prevent toxic behaviors from taking hold and undermining team progress. One of the leaders we interviewed, Samuel, described his strategies for building and maintaining productive, healthy teams with the highly demanding task of dismantling nuclear power plants on very tight schedules in countries around the world.

As vice president of engineering operations, Samuel built a team of American workers and transported them to remote locations where they lived together until the task was complete. Because of these circumstances, he carefully selected workers and monitored them closely while on the job. If there were significant coworker problems, it was no easy task to send someone home and find a replacement when home was on the other side of the world, and there could be weeks of waiting for a replacement. Also, because the work was physically dangerous, the whole team could be put in jeopardy if they had a difficult coworker.

Samuel's actions effectively stopped any emergence or escalation of potentially toxic situations.

The first thing Samuel did was to let his team know that he would not tolerate counterproductive behaviors that sabotaged team progress. Second, he made sure that he walked the talk of fairness and respect to each of his team members. Third, he made a point of checking out the morale or mood of the team on any given day. He asked members, "How are you? How are things going?" and he was interested in their answers. He stopped what he was doing and focused intently on their responses.

Team members were soon looking out for each other in the same way the leader looked out for them. This leader stopped toxicity in its tracks by spreading "respectful care" among his team. The norm was that if a team member needed extra attention or support, someone would go to the leader on his or her behalf if the individual with this need did not. This was not done in a blaming way but in an informative fashion. Samuel would act by going up to the crew member, noting that he understood that things were not going so well, and offering a day off for the individual to sort things out. Although the team had to work shorthanded temporarily, it was preferable to working with someone who was jeopardizing the operation.

Nevertheless, there were still times when toxic behavior ran rampant over the team and Samuel did have to send someone home. Although most leaders don't have the luxury of sending someone home for an indefinite period of time the way Samuel did, our point is that this acknowledgment of the inappropriate behavior, as well as not tolerating it, can work.

One of these situations occurred early in Samuel's career as a manager, when there was no internal appraisal structure that provided honest feedback on team behavior. As a result of this experience, he designed an internal performance appraisal system for choosing team members for special projects. (This is an example of a proactive strategy.) He made sure that he honored the importance of giving specific behavioral appraisals for all his crew members. In other words, he was a caregiver to the team in a direct, honest fashion by calling issues the way he saw them. At the same time, he watched carefully, keeping his ear to the ground and understanding the individuals with whom he worked as well as the system that they created. He solved problems proactively and interpersonally when at all possible. And, when it wasn't possible to solve, he depended on the system to help him act decisively and directly with the toxic person so that his team could carry on safely.

Samuel was a leader who walked the talk of respectful engagement, honest feedback, and caring concern for those with whom he worked.

Reactive Strategies for Dealing with Toxic Teams

The proactive strategies described in the first half of this chapter are about being prepared before toxicity hits. In contrast, the reactive team interventions are about focusing on strategies that will help once you know you have a problem with toxicity. The former is analogous to being vaccinated to ward off the illness before it strikes; the latter is taking antibiotics to fight an existing infection. Figure 6.1 shows the three primary reactive team strategies that can help a leader deal directly with recognizing, analyzing, and intervening with team toxicity:

- Use 360-degree team feedback systems.
- Conduct exit interviews.
- Identify toxic protectors.

Use 360-Degree Team Feedback Systems

Most leaders are familiar with 360-degree leader assessment systems—those processes that provide confidential feedback to leaders from several sources, including the leader's boss, direct reports, and peers. However, we have discovered that most leaders are not aware of 360-degree feedback processes for the team, as opposed to the leader. We have found that using a team assessment tool and follow-up interviews of individual team members, including the leader, can uncover ways in which team productivity and relationships have been undermined.

We have not discovered any instrument designed specifically to uncover toxicity within the team. However, one of the instruments that we have found particularly effective for helping the team create meaningful dialogue around issues of toxicity is the Campbell-Hallam-Team Development Survey (TDS).[4] The TDS is both robust and easy to use. However, like any other 360-degree assessment system, placement of this instrument into the wrong hands can cause much more harm than good, so we believe it must be used with a qualified consultant to facilitate the process. Without skilled interpretation of the results and appropriate facilitation of the team after receiving the results, it is much too easy for the team to lay blame on each other and engage in their own pet theories about team process. We have also discovered that there is a tendency to become defensive about the findings: an external consultant can lend insight objectively into the team's functioning.

The TDS identifies how team members perceive several variables associated with team success. This standardized instrument has been normed on a group of 194 teams with almost two thousand team members. (*Normed* refers to a procedure used to develop an instrument that will give respondents an opportunity to compare their individual responses to the average responses of groups with similar demographics.) According to the instrument developers, facilitators must have a degree in business, psychology, industrial relations, or a related field. For our purposes, it is also critical for facilitators to be experienced in such team perspectives as group dynamics, organizational culture, leadership development, and an understanding of toxic systems.

The TDS has a ninety-three-item survey for each team member and a twenty-three-item survey for up to eight outside observers who are familiar with the team's work. Essentially the team receives evaluations from within the team, through its team members, and from outside the team, through individuals who have opportunities to observe the team as it works.

The survey identifies team strengths and weaknesses to stimulate discussion about the most significant team issues. What makes this team assessment instrument so different and useful from many others on the market is its ability to gather feedback about the team from those who have opportunities to observe it—hence, its 360-degree assessment format.

We find the TDS especially helpful for the following reasons:

- Teams can be assured that they are being assessed first on the basis of benchmarked scores of a normed group of 194 teams. Therefore, they see where they stand against this group.

- Team members can see not only how the entire team scored itself, but they have the opportunity to see how observers viewed them on each of the instrument's dimensions.

The TDS also opens up dialogue about the best and worst of the team. Think of it this way: team members already know some of their strengths and areas for improvement, but they probably do not understand completely the impact of these on overall team functioning. The data gathered using the instrument present a full picture of team operations from within the team and outside it.

Any assessment is only as good as the facilitation that occurs afterward, and we have seen so many opportunities where a team was stuck, riding on its laurels, or even immune to any sort of feedback. So, we caution leaders who use this to make sure that someone skilled in facilitation methods is used. The TDS presents the team with the findings of the survey that they completed, a great way of cracking open the door for some truly genuine and productive discussions. Finally, we have found it is often like holding a mirror up to the team members so they can problem-solve the picture that they have created.

This instrument does not measure toxicity. However, what it does, and does effectively, is to cull out the critical issues arresting team success in any one or more of the nineteen dimensions that it assesses:

Time and staffing	Empowerment
Information	Innovation
Material resources	Team assessment
Organizational support	Feedback
Skills	Rewards
Commitment	Leadership
Mission clarity	Satisfaction
Team coordination	Performance
Team unity	Overall index
Individual goals	

When teams start discussing the reasons for the low scores and toxicity turns out to be one of the culprits, we have seen that toxicity can be exposed rather quickly. For example, one team where we facilitated this process had innovation scores that were extremely low compared to the normed group. It's almost as if the group members were waiting for an opportunity to address their concerns related to the one toxic individual whom they believed was a major factor for the low score here. Of course, other issues cropped up related to what this individual was doing to compromise the team. The positive outcome was that the toxic individual determined that she was no longer contributing to the team, and she voluntarily left the organization within ninety days.

With the use of this instrument on another team, a different result occurred. Here, the data pointed to the fact that the leader was not providing consistent and documented feedback on performance to individual team members. Interestingly, the TDS indicated that feedback was neither effective nor timely from the perspectives of both members and observers. So although there was the perception of a toxic person on this team based on the interviews we conducted, it was not fair to intervene with the person at this juncture because no effective performance management was occurring on the part of the leader. In addition, the team said no coaching on specific behaviors had been conducted. And the team even gave the leader feedback that positive reinforcement must be conducted with the same rigor as negative feedback.

In this second example, we added interviews to the TDS process. We have found these to be a rich source of data that can corroborate the results from the TDS, provide contexts for different views, and enhance the learning from the instrument. In about 80 percent of the cases, we conduct interviews to validate the TDS findings.

You may be wondering what happened to the toxic person in this example. With the leader who now understood the need to use performance management more rigorously, the toxic person's behavior changed. But the change was due to more than the performance management system. The deciding factor, based on feedback we received, was that the team suggested that the performance system be applied to the entire team. And the toxic person? He improved for about a year. Then he left voluntarily because, as he put it, he wanted to go on to bigger and better opportunities!

Conduct Exit Interviews: An Often-Forgotten Action Strategy

We preface our discussion on exit interviews with a case example from our research interviews. We mentioned in Chapter Four that many leaders are unaware that coworkers have been suffering for months, and sometimes years, at the hands of a toxic person. The leader may never be informed directly about what is going on within a team if members are afraid of retaliation or just don't want to be viewed as complainers. And many people make accommodations to handle the problem themselves rather than expose their vulnerability to the toxic person's attacks.

Therefore, leaders need to stay alert to signs of team toxicity and act decisively to stop the behaviors and support the team's healing. There are two areas for the leader to address: the problem and the systemic characteristics of the problem. We begin by introducing George and Belinda.

A Case Study: Exit Interviews Might Have Revealed a Team Leader's Toxicity. George had just been brought in as the CEO of a large national-brand retail company to engage in a large-scale organization change process. When he arrived, he noted that several managers wielded a lot of organizational power that they were using to run their own show. They set their own goals, schedules, and rules for the team. Unfortunately, these managers were invested in keeping the company stagnant rather than moving forward.

One individual, Belinda, stood out from the more typical naysayers, and she reported directly to George. He thought she appeared to be organization-oriented and very people-centered. But relatively quickly, George began to notice that team members from Belinda's division weren't telling him much when he called them to get their opinion or suggestions on a specific change project. It didn't seem to be just disinterest on their part; rather, they seemed terrified to tell him anything of substance, but he couldn't uncover why they might experience such fear.

After an entire year, he finally began to see a pattern of non-compliance and lack of motivation to support any kind of change initiative within Belinda's unit:

> I was a year and a half in the organization, and we had lost a lot of good people before I discovered what was happening below the surface. At first, this person, I'll call her Belinda, befriended me and was supportive. It was really a way of securing her power, but I didn't get it at first. I missed it in the beginning of our relationship until I started to realize that my directives weren't getting done. It was only once I discovered the pattern that I realized a whole system of fear and secrecy was in operation.

It turned out that Belinda was blocking people from bringing reports into open discussion or to George or anyone else in the organization. She controlled her interests through veiled threats to fire people or ostracize them from the unit. People became her loyal followers out of fear—fear of her and fear of change. The best and most marketable employees left rather than suffer under her leadership. The survivors showed up unmotivated and negative about their work, each other, and the organization. George finally fired her to deal with the toxic team situation that infected the entire system with negativity and stagnation. After she left, he said, "People came up to me and said, 'I really wanted to make the changes, but Belinda would not allow it. I wanted to talk to you about the situation, but I was afraid.'"

From our perspectives, George needed to trust his intuition. He knows that he is a seasoned and effective manager of people. If he "sees and hears fear" when he meets with team members, then it is highly likely that fear is present as part of the climate of the team. But he still must determine if the fear relates to his exercise of authority or conditions within the team.

The first step is to investigate the company's policies and values in relation to difficult and toxic behaviors. We would like to hope that he already knew this information when he was hired, but often leaders do not investigate the behavioral norms until they are facing a problem of some magnitude. There is a very high percentage of toxic behaviors in the workplace. Having an organizational system that does not tolerate this type of abuse is a significant component in overcoming long-term effects.

Fear from team members was George's first clue of a problem; his second was that no one on the team was moving ahead with the change initiative. In spite of his best efforts to listen to the team, meet with them individually, and support Belinda, he wasn't able to get movement toward the organizational change goals or encourage team members to speak out. He also had one more clue to the situation: many of the team members who seemed ready to embrace change were leaving. Were they leaving or staying in fear because of change—or because they felt threatened by their team leader for embracing change?

A useful strategy for determining the reasons for self-termination is an exit interview with team members who leave the organization. If the HR department is viewed as supporting values for a respectful organization in all aspects of work, then exit interviews can be used to discuss leadership and management behaviors related to the employee's reasons for leaving. Once George had the information from the exit interviews that HR analyzed into themes, he had hard data on the source of fear in Belinda's team. And if former employees were candid about Belinda's behaviors, then he could deal directly with the source of the problem: the team leader.

Bringing in a Consultant Can Help—But Be Wary! Exit interview data coupled with the 360-degree team assessment are ways to get at team members' perceptions of team functioning. Someone in George's situation might bring in an external consultant to engage in a team assessment process. In addition to the usual vetting of external consultants, it is critical that the consultant be experienced in the system effects of toxicity. She or he needs to be aware of the organization's position on toxic behaviors and how this position is upheld in its policy and culture. If team members are in fear of their toxic boss, they are unlikely to be frank about their situation unless they are assured that the consultant is not working with the boss or would collude in reinforcing the toxic person's authority and behavior.

We write cautiously here with good reason. One of the leaders in our study described a disastrous situation with a consultant who came in to address the dissension in the team. The team members had great hope that the consultant would help them find a compromise with the director and break the cycle of leader secrecy and manipulation. During the course of the training, however, the team discovered that the consultant was reporting to the director all aspects of the work with the team, even information that had been deemed confidential! The consultant in fact had deepened the team's distrust of the leader and strengthened her reputation as a manipulator.

Rebuilding George's Team by Using Team System Assessments. Belinda was finally terminated after a lengthy process. But what happened to the team? They had been living with her for years and had tolerated significant abuse during this time. Although there was an escalation of her secrecy, control, and isolation when George arrived as CEO to spearhead the change effort, the team historically had to bow to her "autocratic commands" and "enforced nurturing." An important component of the TOCS approach is the remedial and preventive work done with a team once the toxic person has left. These strategies include a number of steps that move the team from maladaptive, counterproductive interpersonal relations to more trusting, positive, and engaging behaviors.

An important component of the TOCS approach is the remedial and preventive work done with a team once the toxic person has left.

The people remaining on the team once the toxic person has departed are survivors; they learned adaptive ways of getting around, disappearing, pushing back, or reconfiguring their own agendas. Some members of the team may need individual treatment given the psychosomatic and emotional damage that was frequently reported as a result of dealing with toxic persons at work. However, individual treatment delivered by external providers will not replace the teamwork that must be designed to rebuild trust, communication, and healthy team relations. Decision making, information channeling, and leadership style have all been significant areas of damage in teams infected by toxicity.

Consider the list of ineffective team relations that were reported to us in our study (and listed in Exhibit 2.1 in Chapter Two): just one or two of them are enough to ensure the failure of a project.

Identify Toxic Protectors: The Hidden Enablers

One of the significant discoveries in our study of toxic personalities was the presence of toxic protectors in the organizational system. Just as a bodyguard can safeguard from harm the physical well-being of a person, the protector safeguards the toxic person from harm's way within the organization, with "harm's way" defined as any perceived intrusion on the toxic person's agenda. Sometimes these protectors are peers. Other times they are direct and indirect reports. Even bosses can protect. We have also heard of cases where customers protect because they like the "goods" or "services" they are receiving, so they will put up with an awful lot before reporting the toxic abuse. In addition, protectors are often unaware of their role in encouraging the toxic behaviors.

Protectors are often unaware of their role in encouraging the toxic behaviors.

In the seminars and consultations we have been conducting about toxic work environments, we have observed the "ahas" of self-awareness as clients realize that they have been protecting for a very long time and are astounded that they have allowed this behavior to continue. Toxic protectors emerge in different guises and may or may not be intentionally colluding to empower the toxicity. Stories from our interviews and the findings from our survey identified three conditions that invite toxic protectors: special relationships, the need for power, and the need to maintain productivity.

We also found protectors of the victims, who shielded individuals from the toxic behaviors. We refer to these individuals as *toxic buffers* because they stand between the toxic person and the team. Often they have formed a special relationship with the toxic person and become that person's "interpreter" to others. However, in spite of their good intentions, they inadvertently and indirectly protect a toxic individual from being responsible for his or her behavior.

Our survey identified three sources of motivation for the protectors: special relationships, the need for power, and the need to maintain productivity

---

The protectors of the toxic person have their most powerful and immediate effect at the team level of the organization because they often prevent people outside the team from recognizing the destructive, insidious effects of the toxic person. With a protector in the system, it is a difficult to recognize that the toxic person is spinning a web of destruction, especially by those at a higher level in the reporting structure. The protector's self-proclaimed role is to protect the toxic person from being discovered by those who may have the authority to do something about the situation. This doesn't mean that those who report to the toxic person or those in lateral positions don't see the destruction; rather, they are rendered impotent because the protector is more powerful than they are. Here's an example from our in-depth interviews to illustrate how one of the more complicated protection systems works.

Special Relationship Protectors. John worked as a project manager in marketing in a large Fortune 500 company. He was there for sixteen years in this division, and for twelve of those years, he endured, fought, and was vilified by Jill, director of sales and marketing. Jill was a source of trouble for almost the entire marketing department, but regardless of her incompetence, her actions, and the reports of her toxic behaviors, she held on to the position for twenty years. Why? She was the daughter of one of the top officers in a multimillion-dollar company, so she had protection through a special relationship—in this case, nepotism. It was believed that she couldn't be touched, in spite of the fact that she had relatively weak qualifications for the job.

Jill fired anyone who disagreed with her or whom she felt didn't make her look good. Installing surveillance cameras under the guise of security to find out who was out to get her, she acted on it without explanation once she had the information. John became a target because he didn't cower to her demands.

John still doesn't understand why he ever stayed so long and put up with the unrelenting attack on him and his department. Why did he stay? What kept Jill from firing him? John and his team had the respect of Tim, vice president of sales, who was highly regarded throughout the business. Tim had the positional authority to fire and took the stance that Jill should be fired. But he believed he could not exercise his right to terminate her employment because of her familial connections to the highest level of the organization. John called Tim "the patron as vice president of sales" in his description of the department politics:

> We had a patron as VP of sales. And he was a very, very strong manager. So there was a standoff. She really couldn't mess with us too much as long as he was the VP of sales. In the sales training department, we had about ten people. So the other sixty-some people all worked outside our sales area, and she ran herd over all of them. We were the only department she couldn't screw with.

To change this abusive situation, Tim talked behind Jill's back in disparaging ways, undermined her authority, and sympathized with her victims. He gave protection to units within his span of control. When he left after eleven years, she fired everyone he had protected. Tim was the toxic buffer: by protecting his team and not confronting the situation, he enabled the abuse to continue for years.

This complicated scenario of protectionism, anger, fear, and threat is a tragic example of how an entire system of more than seventy people can devote more than a decade of their lives trying to survive workplace assaults to their dignity. How many of the survivors became toxic themselves in their treatment of coworkers? They survived by being underhanded, manipulative, and sabotaging even positive efforts. Tim assuaged his conscience by protecting a few, sympathizing with victims, and yet not exercising the power he held to make a real difference in the situation. The reason was that the culture led employees to believe that if you had friends at the top, it did not matter how you behaved. No one could touch you.

The lesson here is that protectors can come in many different forms for many different reasons, but protectors do not protect an organization from the tragic human or bottom-line costs of toxicity. In fact, they prolong the situation by making it difficult for others who have the authority to take action, for those who are experiencing the abuse to report it without retaliation, and for organizations to recognize where toxicity is festering. Protectors emerge from systems that don't have a clear and defensible value system that consistently stands up to toxic behaviors.

Protectors do not protect an organization from the tragic human or bottom-line costs of toxicity. In fact, they prolong the situation by making it difficult for others who have the authority to take action.

The special relationship protector is someone with either formal or informal power, who forms a relationship with this individual. This protector goes to bat for this individual at team meetings, supports his or her agenda in large public forums, or provides the data that the toxic person needs to advance his or her agenda. The relationship appears almost as a friendship of sorts. And at times it is. But again, the protector benefits in some way from this relationship.

The special relationship protector is someone with either formal or informal power, who forms a relationship with this individual.

Power Protectors. Another type of toxic protector that we discovered in our research study is the protector who is operating from a need to acquire power or prestige through the toxic person's behavior. For example, the protector's need for power was portrayed vividly in a story told by Monica, a vice president of finance. She became the protector between the president and the other members of the executive team. The president was arbitrary, controlling, and demanding of his team, and he regularly humiliated and insulted them publicly. Most of the executive team would withdraw from any fight with him and go underground with their complaints—all except Monica, who eagerly defended the president and carefully cultivated her relationship with him.

It didn't take long before the president used Monica as his conduit of information to the rest of the team. De facto, she became a powerful second in command. She was able to filter all information in both directions and was greatly rewarded for her protection of the president, to the executive team's disgruntlement. Her protection served her own purposes of gaining power, and the president's purposes of continuing his toxic behaviors unabated.

From our research, we discovered that power protectors are typically at a high level in the organization and are used by the toxic person to promote his or her modus operandi. Why do power protectors do this? First, they are often unaware. They engage in this behavior primarily because they receive something in return, usually a benefit of some sort, such as a completed project, expertise in some arena, or even kudos in group meetings.

Power protectors are typically at a high level in the organization and are used by the toxic person to promote his or her modus operandi.

Productivity Protectors. Our last toxic protector type is a protector who seeks to gain advantage through the toxic person's productivity. This type of protector came up in our leaders' stories of frustration in attempting to terminate a toxic person.

One leader told us there was a three-year period when he and two other directors watched a path of destruction being mowed under their counterpart's unit. The fourth director (of marketing) had a top salesperson, Rob, who micromanaged his team, sabotaged the efforts of other teams in the organization that he saw as threats to his power, and flagrantly abused the organizational value of honest communication. His behaviors and, in particular, the loss of several of his valuable direct reports was a constant source of frustration and gossip with the other directors. The directors couldn't understand why the director of marketing (Rob's supervisor) would not take action—at the very least, to try to curb his behaviors and, at best, to terminate him. Eventually they figured out that this difficult person was producing the kinds of sales that the marketing director was able to report upward as a part of her own achievements. She was well rewarded for the jump in sales during the early years after Rob's arrival, and it was going to cost her plenty (from her view) to lose Rob.

In spite of the organizational values that would back up all of the directors' concerns about Rob's behavior, they didn't think that they could intervene with someone at their same level or go higher to discuss their concerns. It wasn't until Rob's toxicity caused him to lose valuable employees, who were being browbeaten into producing the sales, that the system of protection began to shift. No longer did the director of marketing have the boasts of productivity to protect Rob, and when he was no longer of use to the director, she abruptly fired him.

Intervening with Toxic Protectors. So how can you intervene with a toxic protector? It does not matter the reason that the protection system is operational: special relationships, the need for power, or the need to maintain productivity. Determining the team's modus operandi and the source of the toxic behaviors will uncover the role of the protector. For example, one of the leaders with whom we talked described the conundrum that leaders face when they have a productive person but this person's behaviors are so destructive that deciding whether to keep him or her in the organization has no easy answer:

> I believe leaders struggle when they see this great value these people might bring to the organization, yet on the other hand, they are highly destructive. Leaders want to live in denial that the personality issues that this person has are really as toxic as they are. Therefore, leaders who are more isolated and closed to input have a tendency to be accepting of the bad with the good. But if you are one of those leaders who really want to probe deeply within the organization and really understand everybody's role and really want to find out what's happening among people, then you have much less tendency to allow these toxic people to stay in the organization.

Essentially each of the strategies that we have recommended in this chapter on teams—proactive or reactive—will help pinpoint the protector role in a specific team system. Here are a few steps to take with protectors once you find them.

• *Step 1: Be alert that the role of toxic protector exists.* This person invariably interferes with the overall effectiveness of the team. Therefore, we suggest that the leader conduct periodic, anonymous team assessments. This could be something as formal as the TDS (please refer to page 132 for a review of the TDS) or a survey to determine team members' views on the team's operations—or something as informal as brief interviews with staff. This is not simply to find the toxic protector. Actually it is good leadership practice to conduct periodic team assessments.

They are brief and straightforward, and might pose questions that pertain to areas of achievement, obstacles in the path of effective functioning, and areas for improvement.

- *Step 2: Carefully and judiciously sift through the information that team members have provided.* Make notes on topics, people, and emotions that come up frequently, as well as anything that surprises you about the team. Read over your notes, and identify themes—something that about half a group identifies. Remember, you're not out to find the protector. Your job is to create a more productive team. So look for themes around team norms collaboration among team members, team decision making, informal leadership of the team, and overall team emotional climate. Is there mention of someone who is frequently supportive, or difficult, or a problem solver? You'll likely find positive areas of functioning, and that is great! Moreover, you may uncover areas needing improvement, including obstacles that prevent the team from functioning successfully at full force.

- *Step 3: Give the team feedback on the themes you discover.* Then listen. See if they have some solutions for the areas needing improvement or obstacles that present themselves. If there are some areas that are confidential (for example, relating to the protector), let the team know that there are some confidential items you will deal with directly on your own.

- *Step 4: If there is a protector, talk to the person.* We suggest giving feedback in the same way that any effective performance management systems would dictate. Chapter Seven includes an outline of a model for individual feedback in relation to toxic behaviors.[5] These same principles will serve you well when providing feedback in this situation.

Step 1 in this process is the most important. In working with your team system and uncovering the potential role of the toxic protector, the key element is the identification process. An informal system, where a leader seeks regular feedback from the team, can seamlessly be integrated with your leadership initiatives and performance management procedures. It is a way to keep your ear to the ground.

Certainly, periodic checks of asking around about how things are going are useful. This process can be made a bit more formal by inviting written feedback. At times, leaders have asked us just how anonymous the feedback can be when there are only a few people on a team. It is true that anonymity is reduced in these circumstances. Leaders need to state up front that although the small numbers may not make the respondent entirely anonymous, respondents can be assured that the information will remain confidential and no names will be attached to the responses themselves. All feedback will be given at the level of themes, not quotes or specifics that would compromise anyone's confidentiality. There are always some risks in working with confidential material, but when it is treated with respect, we have found that the benefit of sharing the knowledge gained with the team itself far outweighs the potential risks involved.

Summary of Team Interventions

We have covered a lot of ground in this chapter on team strategies. We have detailed proactive interventions, including team value building with or without organizational values being in place, and reactive interventions, including 360-degree feedback, exit interviews, team system assessments, and strategies for managing the toxic protector. Of course, all of these strategies work better with toxic behaviors when they are implemented in an organization that has a strong focus on values supporting respectful engagement. Nonetheless, working teams are the foundation of productivity in the organization; they are the worker bees of the hive, and it is not wise or realistic to wait for an entire organization to work on values when the team is losing valuable time and resources, both human and financial.

Through our experiences, our research, and the many comments that leaders have reported to us in our consulting practices, we believe that team leaders can be successful in dealing with toxicity as well as improving their relationship with the team by using the strategies offered in this chapter. Our methods do not represent an exhaustive list, and you are likely already engaged in management practices that can easily be adapted to uncovering the toxic system and intervening. Be alert to the presence of toxicity. Understand the underlying issues at the team level. Then act creatively in the best interest of your team.

You may make some mistakes in trying to do what is best for your team. Nonetheless, if your intention is to create a team that operates with respect for others in the organization, who can argue with that purpose in spite of a few missteps? Remember that this team process is gearing your team to the future. And respectful engagement is one significant way to ward off toxicity and reduce the probability of toxic people ever entering your organization again.

Now that we have presented how to manage toxic team dynamics, Chapter Seven describes how to deal with toxic individuals on a one-on-one basis.

7

INDIVIDUAL STRATEGIES

Dealing with Toxic People One-on-One

In situations with a toxic individual, basically I start by just sitting down with the individual, and being very direct about my feedback, letting them know how their behavior is affecting me and others in the organization. I value them for who they are, building them up, and then lay out the specific things they do that are destructive and that could be turned into positives. I try to get them to use their energy in a positive way.

—Quote from study respondent

This quotation from a leader in our study exemplifies an individual intervention. Some might interpret this intervention positively: an appropriate outcome occurred as a result of this feedback. Others might say it represents the futility of trying feedback one too many times. But whatever the case, feedback is likely to be most successful when the systemic components of organizational and team strategies are in place.

This has been the most difficult chapter for us to write because while we want to help leaders deal with a specific toxic person, we know that intervening with this individual alone isn't likely to produce the best results possible. However, by understanding a few important dimensions of individual interventions, it is apparent why sometimes the leader must intervene directly with the individual around the issue of toxic behaviors.

There certainly are times that leaders need to do something right away to halt the behavior of a toxic person. Many of our client leaders have come to us with high expectations that by talking with an individual during performance management discussions, they will be able to reduce the person's toxicity significantly. Moreover, by managing the consequences of the toxic person's actions, they are positive that good results will ensue. This is what we refer to as "talking with consequences." Sometimes it works. Sometimes it doesn't.

This chapter will help you understand when management of the toxic individual is likely to produce the most desired consequences. Just as important, though, we want you to know when to let go of focusing on the toxic individual and start implementing systemic interventions. To this end, we look at interventions in two contexts: the organizational or team systems that are already in place, thus allowing more successful individual interventions, and individual interventions that illustrate approaches for leaders or organizations without organizational and team systems in place.

By no means are we saying that direct intervention with a toxic person is going to fail. The TOCS system strategy is designed to help you work across the three levels of intervention: organizational, team, and individual. In this chapter, we explore this rich mix of variables associated with individual interventions, including what to do about them, how to make them work best for you, and how to deal with the obstacles presented. Increasing the probability of success with individual interventions is a function of organizational plus team interventions.

Increasing the probability of success with individual interventions is a function of organizational plus team interventions.

Finally, note that the organization-wide strategies are proactive strategies. The team strategies use both proactive and reactive approaches. In contrast, individual interventions are primarily reactive because one is responding to a toxic person: these individual strategies are designed specifically to change the behavior of a toxic person.

The key difference between large-system strategies and individual strategies is there is no significant proactive way of dealing with the toxic person when he or she is already exhibiting destructive behaviors. You need to respond to the existing problematic behaviors.

The key difference between large-system strategies and individual strategies is there is no significant proactive way of dealing with the toxic person when he or she is already exhibiting destructive behaviors. You need to respond to the existing problematic behaviors.

The probability of success in dealing directly with a toxic person increases when you apply proactive organizational and team interventions. This doesn't mean you must have organizational and team interventions; it simply illustrates that if you want to reap large benefits from individual interventions, you need organizational and team interventions in place. With this idea in mind, we now take you through specific individual interventions that we believe can work either as linked to wider systems interventions or as solo individually focused actions.

There are four specific, individually designed strategies for working with a toxic person: targeted feedback, performance appraisals, coaching, and termination. Any one or a combination of these actions will likely decrease the probability that the toxicity will spread beyond the immediate situation and inoculate the

Figure 7.1 TOCS Model: Individual Strategies

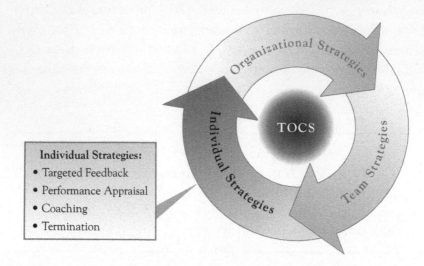

organization, teams, and coworkers against further toxic threat. These TOCS individual strategies are presented in Figure 7.1 and are described in detail in the rest of this chapter.

Strategy 1: Managing a Toxic Individual's Performance by Providing Targeted Feedback

In an organization of zero tolerance for habitual toxic behaviors and where the values are upheld by leadership, thoughtful and targeted feedback within the context of performance management can be effective. This is the best-case scenario for performance feedback with the toxic person. Even without the zero-tolerance and upheld-values perspectives, individual interventions may be effective, though not to the degree if these perspectives were in place.

In an organization of zero tolerance for habitual toxic behaviors, targeted feedback within the context of performance management can be effective.

First, consider something about human behavior that relates to targeted feedback. Some people have such deeply ingrained counterproductive patterns of behavior that short of undergoing psychotherapy (and sometimes not even with psychotherapy), they are unable or unwilling to change. Typically these individuals may elect to quit their jobs rather than undergo any process for individual change. Nonetheless, some will benefit from structured and systematic feedback designed to change specific behaviors in a particular situation. In other words, you won't change their personality, but you might be able to change how they cope with their frustration at work.

Second, good targeted feedback is not an isolated process. It should be integrated with any of the remaining individual strategies we identify in this chapter. In order to really hone in on this strategy, we do separate it here. However, it's likely you'll identify ways to blend targeted individual feedback with the other individual actions we propose.

Any manager has frequent opportunities to give feedback to a toxic person. Nevertheless, before placing too much stock in this method, let's review one of the findings from our research study. Bosses in our study found feedback only somewhat effective in stopping toxic behaviors. And female managers found giving feedback to direct reports much less effective than did male managers. Both men and women did view feedback as the natural reaction to someone who is acting inappropriately, and they expressed discouragement and even insult when their best intentions were thwarted. It is not surprising that many leaders preferred to avoid the toxic person or keep their teams out of harm's way rather than provide targeted feedback.

Female managers found giving feedback to direct reports much less effective than did male managers.

With this in mind, there certainly are ways to increase success through feedback. Targeted feedback should be done with rigor and completeness, as one of our managers emphasized:

> Managers need to remain open to feedback, and when they hear of a people conflict, they should address it right away and hold people accountable for results and value-added work.

It should also be abandoned after a reasonable period of time when it's not working.

Good targeted feedback is an iterative process of information and data to the individual and discussion with him or her. Leaders sometimes misconstrue targeted feedback as associated only with poor performance. Although this is certainly the initial focus with toxic behaviors, we would be remiss in not addressing the important dimension of positive feedback. In any process of feedback, it is important to acknowledge strengths that a person brings to the system. And with a toxic person, a balanced and fair performance process goes a long way in helping that person to be more receptive to the changes required of him or her. We have found that because some toxic behaviors are largely passive-aggressive, starting with the positive can overcome the person's evasive tactics to avoid feedback or retaliate against the leader for not being more encouraging and positive. Thus, even if *you* are more focused on being rid of their most deleterious behaviors, start with the expeditious use of positive feedback focused on the person's strengths. This approach will lay the groundwork of the relationship, so your negative feedback has a chance of being received as constructive suggestions for change.

We teach this basic targeted feedback process to our clients:[1]

Phase I: Identify the Problem

1. Describe the problem as you have observed it.
2. Be clear.
   - Don't infer.
   - Don't use sarcasm.

- Don't use absolute terms such as *never, always,* or *constantly.*
- Avoid judgmental questioning.

Phase II: Use a Sequential Process to Target a Resolution

1. Relate why you perceive this as a problem.
2. Pause to give the individual an opportunity to share his or her views.
3. Get agreement, whenever possible, that a problem exists.
4. Brainstorm alternatives on solving the problem.
5. Agree on one alternative.

Phase III: Provide a Process for Achieving the Performance Goals

1. Outline the next steps.
2. Follow up.

Feedback Phase I: Identify the Problem

For both the nontoxic and toxic person, there is no difference in the first phase of the process: you begin by identifying the problem, which has two critical components.

Describe the Problem as You Have Observed It. As with any other performance you are trying to change, use concrete language that is behaviorally specific. Describe the behavior as either you or others have observed it, being very cautious by not inferring other behaviors. Inferences of any kind can often send a toxic person off the deep end! As from the old *Dragnet* series, "Just the facts, ma'am!"

Be Clear. Many leader actions can get in the way of clarity. One is sarcasm. Don't use it, because this is likely to ignite a flame that will be difficult to extinguish.

Also, don't generalize. Although one of the issues with toxic people is that their behaviors are so inappropriate and have such a powerful impact on those around them, it is easy to believe that they act badly all the time. Thus, leaders have a tendency to use absolute language such as, "You *always* criticize others" or "You *never* help anyone out on the team." Generalizing is likely to cause them to respond in a defensive manner with such answers as, "I don't always do that!" And, in fact, they may be correct; there are times that they don't engage in this behavior. You'll recall that the leaders in our survey reported that toxic persons they knew acted out four or five times a week, so their defensive stance distracts from targeted feedback. Absolute language puts your feedback off track and may trigger a defensive reaction that has a strong tendency to negate the true behaviors you are trying to confront. Therefore, avoid absolute terms when giving feedback.

Finally, avoid judgmental language. Sometimes in the performance management process, a leader has to gather additional information through questioning. Because leaders may be close to the breaking point at this stage, their questioning may become rather judgmental. For example, if there have been complaints from customers that the toxic person raised his voice at them, there's a tendency to question the toxic person in a judgmental way ("Wouldn't you agree that you …"), instead of a more appropriate line of questioning ("What might have caused …"). This less judgmental language is actually more respectful (you are trying to model respectful engagement after all) and doesn't fuel the flames as much, so it is more likely to produce positive results.

Absolute language puts your feedback off track and may trigger a defensive reaction that has a tendency to negate the true behaviors you are trying to confront.

Feedback Phase 2: Use a Sequential Process to Target a Resolution

This phase follows a sequential process to target a resolution to the toxic behavior. Let's look at each step in more detail.

Step 1: Begin the Discussion with Why You Perceive This Behavior as a Problem. This is an opportunity to introduce other data that relate to the toxic behavior, including reports from other teams, feedback you have received from within the team, your own observations, and even feedback from your boss. Whatever relevant feedback you have is appropriate to share. In addition, this is an opportunity to bring in any organizational or team values. Make sure you state how the individual's behavior is an obstacle to the successful realization of these values. One difference during this second phase between the toxic and nontoxic individual is that you don't allow the toxic person to interrupt or interject. If he does, you tell him that he will have an opportunity to speak. You want to finish.

Step 2: Pause and Allow the Individual to Share His or Her Views. This honors the individual's right to address the issue. You may not interrupt or interject, but you may quietly take notes. This will increase the likelihood of suspending judgment. In rare circumstances, we have found a leader to be in error about the toxic behavior, which is why it's important to listen carefully and take detailed notes. And we know that listening improves when one takes notes without attempting to interpret. Difficult as this step is, it's critical because leaders need to be as authentic and reliable as possible in this process. Listening improves authenticity and reliability.

Step 3: Whenever Possible, Get Agreement That a Problem Exists. This can be quite different from how you might handle a nontoxic person. With a nontoxic person, agreement occurs far more frequently than with a toxic person. In fact, with a toxic person, you may not even arrive at agreement.

The main reason for this step is based on one of the results from our research study: toxic individuals are often clueless about their toxicity. To have them face the hard facts of their misbehavior is difficult. Many are not capable of recognizing and acknowledging the problem. So be prepared for an onslaught that you will need to redirect into solving the problem.

Step 4: Brainstorm Alternatives on Solving the Problem. Brainstorming is not just your ideas but includes the ideas of the person you are helping to change. In fact, you may be surprised at the good ideas and good rapport that come from an open process of brainstorming.

Step 5: Agree on One Alternative. Be prepared that the toxic person will probably not want to brainstorm. In this circumstance, you will need to be direct in telling the person what you expect. Be firm but respectful. If agreement isn't possible, you may need to be direct regarding your expectations for future behavior.

Feedback Phase 3: Provide a Process for Achieving the Performance Goals

In the case of toxic behaviors, there must be frequent review of the expectations because of the habitual nature of the person's behavior. For example, think about the process of losing weight: every diet plan encourages you to get on the scale at least once a week to assess your progress and, more importantly, remind you that you are on a diet! For toxic behaviors, a once-a-week routine may not be too frequent an assessment check. This check will act as a reminder that you as a leader are invested in the process, you are serious about this person's change in behavior, and you are there to offer support for change. Information should be collected from key stakeholders as often as needed during this process.

First, outline the next steps, including the consequences that will occur if the expectations are not met. Keep in mind that there's a fine line between consequences and threats. Real consequences have intended repercussions that will occur; in contrast, threats have intended repercussions that you are hesitant about putting into action. Then follow up when you said you would and with the consequences you previously stated.

Critical to this targeted feedback intervention is providing concrete descriptions of what you want to happen. Many leaders are familiar with the SMART model, and we have included it here to help you develop concrete, specific, and accurate behavioral feedback that we have found is critical in this phase:

Specific	Precisely what do you want the toxic person to do?
Measurable	How will you know the individual has met this expectation such that it can be observed and measured?
Achievable	Are you providing expectations that are in the person's realm to accomplish?
Results oriented	Will the potential change in their behavior truly add value to the organization?
Time specific	What is the time period in which this should be accomplished?

Any one of the five areas in the SMART model can be integrated into any of the phases of the targeted feedback model:

- *Specific.* You'll know that your expectation is specific if you ground it in concrete actions. Here, you define what "respectful engagement" means in observable behavior. With some clients, we have found it useful to suggest taking the opposite of what you have been observing. For example, if someone is talking behind someone's back in destructive ways, you may want to turn this around such that one example of respectful engagement is giving someone feedback in the way the toxic person would like to receive it. At this stage, it's important to provide multiple examples to increase the probability that the toxic person understands what is expected. And if you can't extract examples from the individual, then you need to be direct about the specifics of what you expect.

- *Measurable*. Your expectation is measurable if someone not familiar with the individual would know when the behavior changes. It may not be able to be measured in numbers, but it can be measured in the sense that you'll know if it has increased or decreased in intensity or frequency.

- *Achievable*. You do not want to give any expectations that are impossible for an individual to realize.

- *Results oriented*. Your expectation needs to connect with the real work that the individual does and provides worth to the organization. For example, this is a prime opportunity to have results associated with respectful engagement, which brings value to the organization through more effective teamwork.

- *Time specific*. You need to identify a time line for the person to change his or her toxic behaviors.

Remember to stay realistic about the probability of success when using feedback as the sole intervention. It is very difficult to achieve and sustain behavioral change with individuals who habitually use toxic behaviors to achieve their goals and control their environments. In fact, some organizations may opt to take advantage of professional development opportunities to assist their managers in coaching skills needed to work with toxic individuals. However, given the time and skill requirements needed for working effectively with toxic people, leaders may choose to engage a professional executive coach rather than guide the change process themselves.

Strategy 2: Using Performance Appraisals to Integrate Values

Performance appraisal can be effective when it is in alignment with organizational values that support specific behavioral goals for respectful engagement. Much of what we have already covered related to good targeted feedback can be directly applied to performance appraisals, so here we focus on areas of performance appraisal that have not been covered in the targeted feedback area.

Values integration is the benchmark for the best kind of performance appraisal with toxic individuals. When the performance appraisal system addresses values of respectful and honest interchange, the leader has a strong foundation for legitimizing the inclusion of feedback on behavior. In this section, we consider how the manager provides feedback in two different scenarios: one where the values are identified within the organization or team and the other where there are no clearly specified values.

Values integration is the benchmark for the best kind of performance appraisal with toxic individuals.

Feedback During Performance Appraisals When Values Are Clearly Identified

With the TOCS approach, managers are shown how to use feedback in a constructive way that contributes to the overall performance appraisal process. The best way to engage a performance appraisal process with a toxic person is by using multiple assessors, which can be accomplished by using a 360-degree feedback process conducted by an external consultant. The process includes inviting coworkers and key customers to provide feedback directly to the toxic person, including the person's own self-evaluation.

Keep in mind that a self-evaluation is not always very reveal-ing because toxic people are often oblivious to the impact they are having on others and generally point the finger at someone else for their difficulties. In fact, that is part of what makes the process of change so difficult. However, 360-degree feedback processes are only as good as the integrity of the system. In addition, the leader may wish to review the performance appraisals previously con-ducted on this individual in order to discern any kind of patterns and longevity of the toxic person's behavior. There is mounting evidence that 360-degree feedback should be used primarily for developmental purposes. Only when there is confidence in the system and the belief that it provides an accurate snapshot of job-relevant behavior should an organization consider using it for more formal processes, for example, performance appraisal.[2]

Research further indicates that if the process is for devel-opmental purposes, the 360-degree results should not be public data.[3] Essentially this means that only the individual being assessed should be privy to the results—not coworkers, not direct reports, not even the person's boss. One of the main reasons for this level of confidentiality is to prevent the sabotage of the 360-degree process by turning it into a popularity contest in which the toxic person alters her behavior just before the assess-ment process or subtly lets assessors know that their performance appraisal and even their salary depend on the results. These tactics are less likely to occur if the individual alone receives the feedback.

However, there are ways for the leader to integrate the results from the 360-degree feedback into the performance appraisal process, while keeping the 360-degree data developmental in nature. One way to do this is to invite the individual being assessed (in this case, the toxic person) to determine what he or she wishes to share with the boss, if anything at all. Another way is to request that the individual gather informal feedback from others and compare results. This validity check can reduce some of the toxic person's hostility if there is not agreement on the results. But what is important is that you as a leader can also identify themes from the multiple sources of data: from whatever the person wishes to share from 360-degree results, personal feedback results, your observations, and what others have been reporting to you. If the toxic person wishes to share results, that's fine. But there should be no direct or subtle coercion on the part of the leader to find out what the results indicate.

The best way to engage a performance appraisal process with the toxic person is through the use of multiple assessors.

Whenever we conduct 360-degree processes, including the follow-up feedback to the individual being assessed, we recommend that the individuals share the data they consider significant with others (including their boss). For example, we have suggested that they share some surprises, data that corroborate their views, critical actions that they intend to take, and the kind of help they might need from others. As you can see, there are ways to integrate 360-degree processes during performance appraisal time, but probably not to the degree that many managers might believe.

There is mounting evidence that 360-degree feedback should be used primarily for developmental purposes.

Because the degree and type of toxic behavior may vary depending on the context (for example, some toxic persons display inappropriate behavior only to those in less powerful positions), it behooves the leader to collect feedback from key stakeholders: those who have an investment in the individual's effective performance, including team members and even customers. And the leader may want to review previous performance appraisals to see improvements that have been made or areas that have been the subject of past appraisals that are still a problem. Check-up 360 by Creative Metrics systematically guides the leader to follow up on the goals for change that were identified in the 360-degree feedback process.[4] This instrument offers an excellent mechanism to follow up on the person's performance on specific behaviors that have been targeted for change. This type of systematic and consistent follow-up on behavioral change is critical in working with the habitual patterns of toxicity. The leader's own observations of the toxic person's behavior are also significant. The person who is delivering the appraisal may be familiar with the person's behavior in teams and management. If that is the case, then feedback can be given with examples that have been directly observed. With multiple sources and contexts of behavioral information, the data are not coming from a single person or situation.

Some toxic persons display inappropriate behavior only to those in less powerful positions. Therefore, it behooves the leader to systematically collect feedback from key stakeholders.

Because toxic behavior is a habitual pattern of behavior, not merely a bad day, review by key stakeholders should be built into the appraisal system and should not be structured as a particular case event. An appraisal system that regularly gathers data from the key players will keep the leader better informed and the employee well aware of the quality of his or her own relations within the unit or team. It also normalizes the process of providing feedback with a consistent and systematic process that is used not just when there is a problem, thus building in the opportunity for leaders to hear the strengths and growth of team members and not only the complaints.

In general, the following areas apply to performance appraisal processes:

- Collect feedback (by the appraiser) from key stakeholders.
- Set behaviorally specific objectives related to the behavioral change you're seeking from the toxic person.
- Set a time line for periodic review of the toxic individual's progress.
- Include the individual's self-designed professional goals for growth.
- Include behavioral criteria related to respectful engagement.

Feedback During Performance Appraisals When Values Are Not Clear

What can a leader do if the organization or team is without specifically named values related to respectful behavior and immediate action is needed? An effective strategy is to identify some of the pronounced values that the organization lives by; maybe they are not well specified, but they are still operational. For example, we encouraged one of our clients to ask his direct reports, peers, and boss if there was a value that was operational on his team. He found one that he had constantly promoted but was certainly not written down. Almost unanimously, the theme was adopted as a value of teamwork. This leader had incorporated his expectations related to the teamwork value on the toxic person's performance appraisal form. And he did this for all his direct reports in the future as well.

Clearly leaders need to conduct performance appraisals that demand behaviorally specific feedback and goals, reviews from other stakeholders, and periodic meetings on progress—and this is a time-consuming effort that takes skill and patience. For this reason, many organizations have contracted the services of a professional coach to help leaders work effectively within the organization. Coaches are frequently brought into management situations to facilitate a change of behavior in the toxic person and restore harmony in the team.

Strategy 3: Coaching

The International Coach Federation says that "coaching is partnering with clients in a thought-provoking and creative process that inspires them to maximize their personal and professional potential. Professional coaches provide an ongoing partnership designed to help clients produce fulfilling results in their personal and professional lives. Coaches help people improve their performances and enhance the quality of their lives."[5]

Organizational coaching can be traced back to the 1950s, when it was used in conjunction with psychological consultations aimed at improving the performance of executives. In the past twenty years, there has been an explosion of activity in this professional field. Both for-profit and nonprofit organizations frequently turn to coaches to assist in improving employee performance. Coaching is an opportunity to keep knowledge within the organization by improving the skills and leadership of existing employees. It also focuses on developing a person's inherent strengths as well as identifying and planning actions around areas for improvement. It seeks to develop the full potential of an individual within the context of organizational needs and goals. And it seeks to facilitate change in an individual in areas of the organization's structure, culture, and climate, with a focus on individual productivity.

Because hiring the right coach to work with a toxic person is tricky, we created a list of important dimensions to consider. Even if the organization has a predetermined list of coaches from which leaders are to choose, you still have two options:

- Interview a potential coach from a predetermined list to see if he or she can fulfill these criteria. This applies to an external coach or one from within the organization (usually from the human resource department).

- Do not use any predetermined coaches, and instead hire your own.

A coach who is being hired to work with a toxic person must meet these criteria:

- Understands the bidirectional process in which both the individual and the organization are taken into account, including the organization's systems, values, and norms, and be willing to incorporate these into the coaching process
- Works with individuals who are highly resistant to change
- Works within the boundary of accountability to the organization
- Assesses information from multiple key stakeholders
- Disbands the coaching effort as soon as there are strong indications that coaching will not work
- Takes time to understand how the organization works and can make recommendations for placement of the individual in other employment within the organization
- Makes recommendations as to how the toxic person's coworkers need to adjust for effective reintegration of the toxic person to the team and to bring in a team consultant if needed in this process

The Coach Needs to Use a Systems Approach

Whether the coach is contracted by the larger organization for any number of employees or individually by the leader of the toxic person, the coach contracted should understand the significance of the organizational system, values, and norms in which the toxic person is operating. This is a bidirectional perspective of the coaching process, incorporating both the individual and systems interventions we have been addressing thus far.[6] Note that some coaches do not embrace a systems view and consequently do not take into account the role of organizational culture, policies, and values that are critical to understanding the toxic person's difficulty in the workplace. This is *not* the kind of coach you need in this situation!

The Coach Needs to Be Prepared to Work with People Who Resist Change

In dealing with habitual toxic behaviors, the coach must be prepared to work effectively with individuals who are highly resistant to change. You may be thinking that this is a no-brainer (of course, they must!). However, some coaches refuse to work with individuals who are highly resistant to change—and with good reason, because they have been burned in the past by getting nowhere with them. However, with this systems perspective (and, in particular, organizational or team values in place), this resistance to change can be mitigated through the reinforcement of consistent behavioral goals at individual, team, and organizational levels.

The Coach Needs to Be Accountable to the Organization

Coaches who work with toxic individuals have an obligation to be accountable for identifying and achieving coaching goals that are relevant to both the individual with whom they are working and the organization or leader hiring them. In aligning these individual and organizational/leader goals, it is critical that coaches understand that they must balance accountability to the organization and responsibility for individual care to the person receiving coaching.

You have every right as a leader to ask the coach to report results. However, be aware that coaches have every right to put limits on what they will report, and this can turn into a negotiating process. A coach is bound by professional ethics that guide the determination of what can be divulged regarding client information in order to maintain effectiveness and trust in the relationship. The organization has a vested interest in the appropriateness and progress of the coaching process. Many times the organization is paying the coach's fees and wants to be assured that change is achievable. Reputable coaches will balance the need for confidentiality with accountability to the organization. They will keep both the client and the organization informed of progress on coaching goals and the likelihood of behavioral change.

The Coach Needs to Assess Information from Multiple Stakeholders

To increase coaching success in working with a toxic individual, coaches must be skilled in assessing significant components that will identify the extent and characteristics of the problem behaviors as they occur in various contexts. Remember that many toxic people are typically chameleon-like and adjust their performance to their audience.

Although different coaches will have their own specific approaches to assessment, the Systems Approach to Coaching Leaders (SACL) recommends that an organization contract coaches who assess the individual and gather information through interview or formal assessment inventories from all internal stakeholders.[7] Following is a list of the multiple sources of information that we have used with our own clients:

- The client being coached
- The manager to whom the toxic person reports
- Direct reports of the toxic person
- Team members
- Customers

- Appraisal reports
- HR reports

Furthermore, the SACL approach trains coaches to analyze the information that they receive in relation to seven important areas of the coaching relationship:

- The organization
- The client
- The client's team or customer
- The coaching relationship
- The coach himself or herself
- The developmental learning tasks for the client
- The best-practices approach for coaching intervention

Each of these areas plays a role in the way the coach and the client establish relevant and realistic goals aligned with organizational values that are consistent with the client's learning needs.

Coaching can be successful, and all parties benefit when there is a strong working relationship among the organization, the coach, and the toxic person; this is a process that is accountable in behavioral terms to all parties. However, in spite of the potential benefits of this strong relationship, it is unlikely that success will be a complete transformation of the client's personality. Nonetheless, the coach's and client's focus on behaviors that damage working relationships, the self-monitoring of such behaviors, and regular feedback on performance can keep some toxic behaviors in check.

The Coach Should Be Aware When Coaching Won't Work

It is possible that the toxic person may not want to pursue goals relevant to organizational objectives that will involve any change in the behaviors identified as problematic. Not surprisingly, the coach may find that the client denies any wrongdoing and blames the organization, the team, or boss for any charges levied at them. At this juncture, the coach, the organization, and possibly the toxic person must make a critical decision as to whether coaching can be effective from the organization's perspective. If coaching is not the answer, several options are left for the leader to consider in managing the toxic person:

- The organization may terminate the coaching contract and pursue a dismissal process.
- The coach may terminate the contract with the organization and contract individually with the toxic person outside the organization.
- The client may choose to terminate coaching and seek alternative employment.

Any of these options might be the ultimate decision when the toxic person is clearly unwilling to work on changing his or her workplace behavior.

The Coach Should Recommend Reassigning a Toxic Individual

Coaches who have done a thorough assessment may also recognize that the toxic person might fit more easily into other types of organizations or perhaps other positions within the organization. Here is where the coach's attention to the organization's structure, culture, and characteristics can make a substantial contribution. By understanding the strengths and difficulties of the person with whom he or she is working, as well as the organizational needs, the coach may make useful suggestions regarding the types of positions that might maximize the resources the individual brings and minimize the impact of inappropriate behaviors that are difficult to change. The coach must be willing to spend time to understand the organization and the multiple venues available for alternative work opportunities there for the toxic person.

Options when coaching is no longer working: the organization terminates the contract and pursues a dismissal process, the coach may terminate the contract and contract independently with the toxic person, or the toxic person terminates coaching and seeks alternative employment.

In our research, leaders in a position to reconfigure the situation around the toxic person found reassignment only somewhat effective. However, the reconfiguring had more to do with taking away or avoiding the assignment of responsibilities to the toxic person. With coaching, the objective is to maximize a person's potential and help him or her remain within the organization in some capacity. None of this is easy to accomplish, and an effective, wise, and patient coach with a solid grounding in organizational culture and values is needed in the process. Of great significance to the success of coaching is the person's desire and motivation to change and willingness to work within the system.

The Coach Should Help Reintegrate the Toxic Person into the Team

The SACL approach includes the customer or team as a critical consideration in designing any coaching intervention with the client. The coach needs to be sensitive to team dynamics and realize that positive change from a toxic team member or leader can upset team norms and raise anxieties. Even when the team gets the change they asked for, the outcome can be disturbing because it requires a change in their past response to the toxic person. From our consulting work, we have heard numerous stories that uncover vividly the web of toxicity in teams.

One manager told us that she had worked diligently to change a team leader's manipulative behaviors and improve the toxic person's relations with his team. The team leader, who had created a great deal of anger and resentment in his team, found that even when he was straightforward with the team members, they continued to distrust him. In fact, they went to the manager and claimed that he was just trying to manipulate them by pretending to change his ways. She couldn't win either way. Of course, the coached client concluded that there was no reason to make the effort himself, and clearly the responsibility for the poor relationship rested with the team.

We see this situation differently. The team, after years of being manipulated by the team leader, was not going to trust him after one month of good behavior. Furthermore, one of the ways in which the team had adjusted to his leadership was to "love to hate him." They had bonded around protecting each other from his leadership and actually received a lot of secondary gain by voicing their anger to others with respect to the toxic person. Thus, to accept him as a good guy would jeopardize their common goal and sense of belonging.

This is where a systems perspective to coaching is critical. Although the manager is making good progress with the team leader, the team needs to develop more constructive ways to connect with each other than having a common complaint. The systems coach will know to bring in a consultant to help build productive working relationships and gradually adjust the team's expectations of the toxic person.

Strategy 4: When All Else Fails: Terminate the Toxic Individual

The most common individual strategy reported in our study was termination of the toxic person. Over and over again, we heard a resounding chorus: "Just get rid of them." Yet "getting rid of someone" is not only difficult to accomplish in a fair and equitable way; it is a long, arduous, and time-consuming process, particularly if there is no organizational system to support the action. Therefore, we have held off discussing termination until the end of this chapter because termination is typically the culmination of failed attempts at any of the other strategies. There is one exception: when the toxic person's behaviors are so severe as to warrant immediate termination.

To make sure that termination is a fair process, a systems approach to toxicity needs to be considered. We'll continue the story of George and Belinda (introduced in Chapter Six) as they move to the last stage of their working relationship. The conclusion of their relationship illustrates a typical process of termination without the benefit of a systems approach to toxicity.

The leader, George, realized finally what was going on in Belinda's unit and began a process of confrontation. He outlined to her the way in which she was falling considerably short of the change initiative goals. At least here, he felt on safe ground because he had the numbers to prove his point. However, Belinda quickly began to point the finger at others who, she said, were responsible for her team's poor showing. She boldly implicated George by suggesting that it was his "failure of leadership" that resulted in the stalling of the change initiative.

She continued her stonewalling until George made it very clear that he was not afraid to challenge her position and that her job was in jeopardy. Belinda quickly changed her tactics and started acting almost reverential toward him, agreeing with every suggestion but still not producing any evidence of follow-through with the team. In fact, team members continued to leave, and Belinda's unit made no substantial progress.

Ultimately Belinda was terminated, but not before a year and a half of change effort had been under siege, supporters of the change had left, and an entire unit had lived in fear of speaking up. George held the formal authority to hire and fire as long as due process was honored, but he did not have a performance appraisal structure or process that addressed Belinda's destructive leadership behaviors. He made the case for termination based on the team's substandard productivity. Unfortunately, the entire team was implicated in the failure.

Here's how the use of the TOCS approach might have prevented the financial and personal damage that resulted from thirty years of Belinda's reign of terror:

1. The organization would have engaged in a process that involved the alignment of values and leadership to a culture of respectful behavior among all employees.

2. Clear and behaviorally specific guidelines that addressed an employee's interpersonal behaviors as a part of performance appraisal would be in place.

3. There would be skip-level evaluations that would allow members of a unit or team to give performance feedback to their supervisor's boss regarding the supervisor's behavior without fear of retaliation.

With these system components in place, the members of Belinda's unit would not have to wait until the CEO (two steps removed) recognized the deception that was undermining his efforts. Remember that Belinda was confident that she could hold the castle under siege, because she had reigned with confidence for thirty years. It wasn't until she felt her job was in jeopardy that she even tried to change. Why? There was no system arsenal to support her direct reports in flushing her out. The CEO's ultimate actions of confronting her directly and consistently on her inappropriate actions would occur in the context of a performance appraisal and would occur much earlier before the rest of the team had left.

When we asked the leaders in our study to describe their organizations' most effective reactive measures, the most frequent response included early confrontation and effective follow-through on consequences. Here are some examples of their recommendations:

- "Confront the behavior as soon as it occurs, and reflect it back to them."

- "Engage in constant communication and immediate feed-back when a toxic issue arises. And holding ground and not letting the person continue to behave in such a nega-tive way."

- "Have consistent follow-up (with dates) with very clear expectations. We have now gotten to where we have severed his employment. He verbally resigned and we accepted. He wanted to take it back and we did not accept that."

The Critical Importance of Formal Authority

Critical to the success of the individual interventions discussed in this chapter is the person who is executing the intervention and his or her position in relation to the toxic person. As we learned from our research study, the effectiveness of giving feedback or reconfiguring a situation depends on the toxic person's position as a peer, direct report, or boss. The leader's span of authority will make a significant difference on the toxic person's willingness to respond to any individual intervention. Because so much of a toxic person's approach to relationships is defined by the need for and exercise of power, many are very attentive to another person's exercise of power through their own position. Whether the toxic person is actively or passively hostile, these behaviors emerge from needs of recognition, control, or dominance.

Thus, in any individual strategy, the person who is exe-cuting the intervention—whether internal or external to the organization—must have sufficient formal authority to carry clout and strong organizational support for taking action. Our research findings were very clear that individual interventions had little or no possibility of succeeding except under these conditions. Although numerous books espouse the virtues of confrontation, manipulation, or evasion in response to a toxic person, without the alignment of organizational values, team norms, and formal authority, the toxicity will continue, and the victims are the ones who will pay the highest price for any action taken.

So for any intervention, it is imperative that leaders under-stand the significance of their own authority and the power attributed to them. For example, if the intervention is to be conducted by a team leader who is responsible for a project but doesn't have the authority to hire, fire, and conduct performance appraisals, there needs to be another person with the authority to oversee the progress and outcomes of the individual intervention. This comment from our open survey confirms the importance of leverage through the authority to exercise consequences:

> The best way to deal with this person was to get someone who had more authority involved to talk to them ... and if their behavior didn't change, then there would be consequences. And these consequences were followed through, which eventually led to this person's termination from the job.

For any intervention, it is imperative that leaders understand the significance of their own authority and the power that is attributed to them.

Conclusion

Can individual interventions create sustainable change of toxic behaviors? Our response is a qualified yes, under these conditions:

- The interventions are conducted within an organization that has clear consequences for toxic behaviors—whether they are exhibited by team leaders, managers, or their top executives.
- The performance appraisal system includes behaviorally specific criteria for respectful engagement.

- The manager or coach uses a consistent, systematic feedback plan that includes the views of all relevant stakeholders, such as managers, skip-level managers, team members or leaders, and coworkers.

When these conditions are in place, the opportunity for success increases greatly. Remember where we began this discussion. It's about increasing the probability of a successful individual intervention.

The person whose behavior is targeted needs to understand that the organization is serious about its commitment to respectful behavior. Individuals who choose not to conduct themselves in accordance with this value will no longer be welcome. It takes effort, commitment, and courage to implement a plan of this scope and intensity in the organization. At the individual level, it is particularly strenuous because a person who is known to be difficult, manipulative, and verbally abusive must be confronted and handled with fairness and equanimity. In most cases, this will take a skilled professional such as a coach, a human resource professional, or an industrial organizational psychologist to assist leaders in developing and implementing an intervention plan. This plan may seek termination through due process, rehabilitation of the person, or appropriate reassignment.

Whatever the final resolution, the changes made will have an effect on all stakeholders: all those who have suffered, questioned, and wondered why nothing was ever done in the past. The effect will include relief, but it also may include a period of guilt, aimlessness, or even loss. These aftereffects need to be recognized and addressed as one part of the TOCS method.

We end this book in the next chapter with a holistic perspective by debunking myths associated with toxic personalities, providing processes for healing, and creating truly positive communities of respectful engagement.

8

MYTHS AND TRUTHS ABOUT TOXICITY – AND RENEWAL FROM A TOXIC ENVIRONMENT

How to Move Beyond Toxicity

Effective organizations pay close attention to both what gets accomplished and how it gets accomplished. In our organization, leaders know that the way they achieve their results is as important as the results themselves, and because of that, our core values are consistently reinforced and upheld. We work hard in the hiring process to ensure a potential team member's fit with our culture. Being open to different perspectives, collaborating effectively, and taking accountability are all critical in our performance-driven culture, so we want to ensure that the people we hire have those natural abilities and can thrive in that kind of environment.

—*Gregg Steinhafel, president and CEO, Target Corporation, July 2008*

Gregg Steinhafel emphasizes the critical significance of lived values of respectful engagement as integrated into the fabric of what team members do every day. Throughout this book, we have uncovered the complexities of dealing with toxic personalities and their systems of power at work. The core of our TOCS model is the implementation of strategies to create a respectful culture at every level of the organization and support a healthy and productive working community.

We have shared the erroneous assumptions many leaders have made about working with these personalities. We devote the first section of this final chapter to debunking the prevalent myths of toxic personalities and, based on our research and experiences, reframe these myths. Some of these myths will probably be a reminder of what you have already read in this book or already know about toxic personalities. Other myths may cause you to pause and reflect because they are counterintuitive. However, even with the most counterintuitive of myths, we hope you will recognize their validity, based on the research we have presented to you, and reframe your perspectives.

The second part of this chapter provides a context for renewal for both the leader and the team. Even when a systemic intervention has been successful, there remain people who have lived through the nightmare and survived the ordeal. Over the previous seven chapters, we have detailed the negative repercussions and systems solutions to toxicity. In this chapter, we focus on leaders and teams who are ready to move forward and renew their commitment to a healthy workplace. Renewal in this context is about taking the human condition in the workplace and making it into something that inspires, provides hope, and gives meaning to people's lives. It affirms an organization's commitment to creating a respectful, energizing, and dignified place for people to work.

The TOCS model of systemic interventions provides a foundation for leaders and teams to renew and invest in building a culture that honors these values. By examining the system of toxicity, identifying concrete behaviors for change, setting appropriate expectations, and giving relevant and inclusive feedback, leaders will demonstrate the power of respect to both individuals and teams. In the second section, we address the significance of renewal through organizational processes that will move people forward in a confident and constructive direction.

Myths and Truths

Following is a list of the myths that every leader should be aware of before they initiate any change practices in their organization related to toxic personalities:

- *Myth 1*: Don't mess with the success of toxic people.
- *Myth 2*: Toxic persons know exactly what they are doing.
- *Myth 3*: Give them feedback, and they will change.
- *Myth 4*: Most people won't put up with toxic behaviors.
- *Myth 5*: Human resources and other consultants solve the problem.
- *Myth 6*: Fire them to resolve the issue.
- *Myth 7*: Toxic behavior is a solo act.
- *Myth 8*: When hiring, seek a little extra competence over a little extra likability.
- *Myth 9*: Bosses see the systemic effects.

These nine myths provide an integrative summary of our research findings and practice recommendations for dealing with toxicity. We hope they will lead you to new insights about your own workplace and the people with whom you work—both toxic and nontoxic.

Myth 1: Don't Mess with the Success of Toxic People

In our research study, we discovered a perception that because some toxic people are high performers, you shouldn't interfere with their success. Of course, we know now that the cost the organization pays for even those who are performing at a high level is often hidden from view. The financial and emotional damage they wreak can set an organization back in reputation and profit in spite of the apparent productivity of some toxic people. And although profit is not a goal of nonprofit organizations, the loss of financial contributions from potential donors is a price these organizations often pay because of toxic employees.

Surprisingly, there was a difference in perceptions about the productivity of toxic personalities, depending on whether the toxic person was a direct or indirect report. We discovered that leaders who had toxic personalities reporting to them saw them as successful more often than if the toxic person was their peer or boss. Many leaders perceive toxic individuals as successful because the toxic person behaves appropriately in their presence and covers their path of destruction from those above them. Their success was attributed to a variety of domains: marketing, sales, and unique knowledge and skills. These are just some of the many results leaders reported that the high-achieving toxic personalities have brought to their organizations. So with improvements like these, it's no wonder that many organizations enable counterproductive behaviors to continue.

Why upset the apple cart with positive organizational results that a toxic individual brings to the organization? This is the sentiment many leaders face until the toxicity begins to affect business results. Many leaders are now asking if high performance is enough, given the devastation these people cause to their coworkers, customers, and the bottom line. One director of a medical device corporation whom we interviewed told us:

> Sarah [fictitious name] built a better clinical organization than her predecessor. However, in spite of her technical competencies in revamping the organization, she isolated people from each other by taking authority away from project leads. She further took decision-making authority away from directors of the various business units, even though she had all the right stuff in terms of her own technical capabilities.

Myth 2: Toxic People Know Exactly What They're Doing

Believe it or not, many toxic individuals are clueless about the effects their behavior has on the organization and those around them. In fact, if you were to confront them about their more obvious transgressions, we predict you would hear two types of responses. First, there's a high likelihood they would respond with indignation: "Well, if you had more concerns about this organization, you'd be backing me up 100 percent." Or: "I seem to be the only one who has the guts to stand up in this situation. The rest of you just don't have the same commitment that I do." Second, there's often a sense of self-righteousness about their actions. They often believe they are the only ones who truly care about the organization and are willing to walk their talk. One CEO reported:

> She [the toxic individual] believed that what she was doing was right for the organization. In fact, she got extremely self-righteous and so much so that she bulldozed others who stood in her way in terms of what she felt the organization needed. And then when I called her to my office to tell her she was being dismissed, this was the first time she "got it" with her response to me of, "Oh, my . . . I'm being fired." She then told me, "I'm not speaking with you because of the disrespect you are showing me."

In essence, while toxic people are often self-interested and self-righteous, paradoxically they are other-directed when it comes to understanding their own behaviors. With few exceptions, wrong-doing is about others, and hardly ever about themselves. These kinds of comments are related to a narcissistic perspective on the world. Toxic persons often cannot find fault in themselves and are shocked if anyone criticizes them. This is the reason that explaining their behaviors to them often doesn't work. This characteristic leads to the next myth.

Myth 3: Give Them Feedback, and They Will Change

Knowing that some toxic personalities are clueless about their toxicity, you can probably understand why feedback doesn't *always* work. We italicize *always* because there are no absolutes when dealing with human behavior. In some contexts, feedback is going to be effective. However, the point of this myth is that many leaders only use feedback strategies without any evidence of change. They either need to give up on these or do something to make the feedback work.

Let's first address when to give up on feedback. Obviously if the person is clueless about his or her toxicity *and* you have tried giving feedback and it doesn't work, you have two options. First, check that your feedback is concrete and behaviorally specific. For example, rather than saying, "Your attitude is really poor at team meetings," say, "I noticed that at meetings you interrupt a fair amount of the time, you attack people who don't agree with you, and you're on your BlackBerry 25 percent of the time." See the difference? It's much more difficult to argue hard data. Even more importantly, it's much more respectful to provide the individual with honest, direct feedback.

Nevertheless, you still may run into frequent roadblocks with the toxic person not accepting what you are saying by arguing and defending his or her actions. If this occurs, you may want to divert to your second option, which is a hard-court press: using a comprehensive performance appraisal by seeking feedback from relevant stakeholders. Or seek a coach from inside or outside the organization to work with the individual.

Investing in these solutions is a big commitment in time, energy, and money, so be clear on your goals for the person and how he or she contributes to the overall goals of the organization. In other words, make sure that the costs are well worth your investment in the person. We know that many leaders have seen this kind of performance management process or something similar. Use the performance feedback system with which you are most comfortable. Obviously this is far easier than looking at the wide-range system components. Individual feedback is a good place to start, but be cautious about spending too much time on giving feedback because the probability is high that it won't work.

As we have related throughout this book, understanding the systems components is most likely going to provide the most leverage in dealing with the toxic person. Therefore, when you are flying solo with the feedback, establish a self-imposed time line for change. If nothing is different in the toxic person's behavior, then it is time to move to a systems strategy for action.

Myth 4: Most People Won't Put Up with Toxic Behaviors

People will put up with toxic behaviors for years and for many reasons: the toxic person may be a high performer or may have a relationship with someone with influence, or someone may be afraid to tackle this individual for fear of being humiliated. Whatever the reason, many people will put up with toxic behaviors for a very long time, even up to thirty years, as one of our respondents noted.

Many people will put up with toxic behaviors for a very long time, even up to thirty years, as one of our respondents noted.

We have found that this myth gets debunked when victims understand the iceberg metaphor. Victims need to weigh the aftermath of destruction caused with the benefits of doing nothing. We have helped our clients understand the significance of this metaphor by going to a dry-erase board and drawing a picture to represent it. Above the water is the tip of the iceberg: the toxic person and the "benefits" of doing nothing. Below the waterline is the huge chunk of iceberg with all the ramifications of the havoc the person is causing the organization, the team, or individuals. Add the positives together; do the same with the negatives. When you discover whether benefits or damages win out, take action.

Myth 5: HR and Other Consultants Solve the Problem

The best response we can provide to this myth is, "Not necessarily." When these professionals realize that there needs to be a threshold when feedback is no longer working and that there needs to be a systemic focus, then, and only then, is the intervention likely to be successful. However, what many HR professionals seem to do is spend far too much time on the feedback component. Please don't misinterpret what we're saying. First, we believe these highly trained HR professionals can truly add value in dealing with toxic individuals. But even they can find themselves entrapped by the toxic system.

> Highly trained HR professionals can truly add value in dealing with toxic individuals. But even they can find themselves entrapped by the toxic system.

Second, success is also about having a system of organizationally identified and enacted values that are precise and clear. These professionals can provide context for this to occur in the organization because they often have the ears of those in power to influence the culture of the organization. For example, in the following quotation from our interviews, the managers who were dealing with the toxic behaviors went to HR for help in creating a corrective plan. They discovered that several complaints had already been made, and HR was able to put together a process that the person accepted. This systematic and multipronged effort was one of the rare situations where providing feedback worked:

> We [managers], after having many informal coaching sessions with him [the toxic person], decided that we needed to put a plan together. So HR wrote up a plan of corrective action. They had initially gotten involved because they had interviewed different people in the department because of some complaining about the comments that this toxic person had made. HR was able to engage him in this plan and speak to him directly without making him feel terrible. He began to work on the plan and we sent him to a training class on how to handle frustration and how to work with people as a part of the plan.

Myth 6: Fire Them to Resolve the Issue

One might think that terminating employment will resolve the issue because it appears to sever the problem at its root cause: the toxic person. However, removing the toxic person doesn't take care of the toxic environment that this individual has created. So when the firing occurs, leaders are often astounded that the problem does not go away. Typically people around the toxic person have amassed a variety of enabling behaviors that allowed the problem to continue. When the toxic person is gone, the learned enabling behavior may persist.

We're not saying that firing is inappropriate. Rather, it often does not accomplish the goals for which it was intended. Leaders think that once the toxic person is gone, the work environment will immediately be healthy. In fact, a healthy environment doesn't necessarily re-emerge miraculously.

Think of it this way. In psychological terms, there is often an "identified patient," say, an alcoholic parent in a household. The entire household has enabled this alcoholism to continue in such ways as making excuses as to why the parent hasn't showed up for a school function or the alcoholic's partner calling the employer saying that this individual is "sick" and won't be at work. When the alcoholic individual stops the drinking, the rest of the family is often left with the ravages of the alcoholism, with questions like, "Who will I take care of now, since much of my life has been spent focusing on this issue? Does this person still need me now that he is much more independent?"

It's the same thing in a toxic work environment. Firing the individual is not the complete answer, and it often doesn't take care of the debris field left by the toxic individual because selected system components have not been addressed. The devastation caused is not just in the work environment: sometimes the toll experienced by others who work with toxic individuals carries over into their home environments. One of our leaders, who had worked for a highly manipulative CEO for two and a half years, described his total obsession with uncovering her (the CEO's) destruction of trust and productivity. Every night he brought home more stories of her duplicity until this toxic boss became the center of his family life. His rage and frustration found expression only at home because he could not safely express himself at work. His rage was directly related to the toxic person whom he believed was ruining his work and personal life, as this quote provides testimony to:

> It was Christmastime. I was trying to put the tree in the stand and the darned thing wouldn't fit. So I went out into the garage and got a hammer, and I went in the living room, hammering this thing, and my wife came in, and she said, "Either you leave that place, or I'm leaving you."

Myth 7: Toxic Behavior Is a Solo Act

By now you probably realize that this is a myth. The toxic person often involves an entire system, pulling others down in a path of destruction. Furthermore, there may be a protector who enables these behaviors. Many leaders assume that the toxic person is a narcissistic, ego-centered control freak who wields power that freezes many in their tracks. This may be true for some. But no matter what the behavior, the uncanny truth is that toxic personalities often don't do this alone. It's likely that someone shields this individual from others, and this individual is the protector.

Protectors often are not aware that they are engaging in this behavior. Instead, they view the outcomes of the toxic person as paramount, whether these are increased organizational profitability, better client service, more effective patient outcomes, enhanced service to a community, or something else. Indeed, the protector—as the toxic buffer—may also try to protect others from the toxic person's behavior, keep the toxic person in place, or simply gain the benefits of the role of rescuer.

Myth 8: When Hiring, Seek a Little Extra Expertise over a Little Extra Likability

We know from research that this is definitely false. We are not saying that expertise should be overlooked. Indeed, it is critical. And to really hone in on the fact that you need to make sure you are hiring competent individuals, we suggest that your selection criteria should be codesigned by staff and managers—the stakeholders who have a vested interest in the success of the hiring outcome.

Second, when designing hiring criteria, the team should be sure not to overlook one criterion that is often forgotten: what psychologists refer to as the likability factor. Given that several candidates' expertise and likability (that is, the positive perception the interviewer has of the candidate) are about equal, choose a little more likability over a little more competency. This does not mean the organization should hire an incompetent person. Rather, if one candidate has a bit more competence than the other one but the other candidate has a bit more likability, hire the candidate with a little less competence and more likability. The small difference in expertise could be addressed with good training later.

Third, conduct behaviorally focused interviews that consider actual, not hypothetical, work situations. With this model, bluffing (and actually lying) becomes close to impossible, because the process is based on facts, not feelings. Essentially, there is a tremendously increased probability that with the involvement of all key stakeholders and as early as possible, colleagues will be much more supportive of this person. Interview questions should be codesigned by key stakeholders; they should be conducted by management and staff as appropriate. Staff interviews can certainly be a group interview of the final candidates. Or there could be one or two staff members who interview; leaders could also interview the candidates separately. However, the organization needs to ensure that all individuals who participate in the interview process are able to confer about their observations regarding the candidate.

Myth 9: Bosses See the Systemic Effects

Of all the groups we have studied (bosses, direct reports, and peers), the boss is the least likely to see the systemic effects of a toxic person. What seems to be occurring is that either people are reluctant to give bosses feedback on what they are observing or the boss is so seduced by the toxic person's productivity or obsequiousness that he or she simply is blind to the need for change. The boss, more than others, appears to be immune to the devastation being caused throughout the system by this one individual. This quote from a vice president in a large corporate environment describes the situation precisely:

> Well, it was challenging, to say the least, because it was a situation where many of us saw the behavior, and many of us were painfully aware of how destructive that behavior was, but because this individual was a peer of ours, we were not able to confront him; and the person's direct boss was obviously tolerating the situation because the numbers coming out of his area still looked good. So we just had to deal with it. Because as a peer, we would observe and we would see, and we would hear all the destructive things that were going on within that person's area of influence, but we weren't directly affected day in and day out, but we were indirectly affected fairly regularly.

In general, when we are consulting with clients, we advise that bosses need to be at the ready to receive any kind of negative feedback—that is, bosses should let people know that they want to hear what's going on, whether it's negative or positive. Then the boss, once hearing particularly negative feedback, needs to make sure he or she doesn't belittle the messenger in the process.

Fostering Renewal from Toxicity for the Leader and Team

Knowing the myths and truths surrounding the toxic person in the workplace puts the leader in a position to prevent or stop the spread of toxicity. The final consideration in warding off the toxic person's presence in your organization includes developmental opportunities to transform practices related to respectful engagement at all levels of the organization. We call this process renewal, and it has two purposes:

- To create an organization that operates with values supporting human dignity with a focus on respectful engagement
- To respond to the ravages created by toxic personalities through a healing process

The first is a proactive process; the second, a reactive one. The proactive method is one of designing the kind of organization with the values that show human respect by not allowing toxicity to fester and spread. The reactive process is about working with those who have been damaged by this toxicity and responding in ways that support individual and team healing.

We have a deep conviction that organizational interventions that are in alignment with the values of the organization have the greatest potential to make an impact and create change. This book is about creating sustainable change that transforms the leadership of an organization to consider the human and financial value associated with respect. In relation to toxicity, the greatest opportunity for renewal is through leadership and team development. Thus, we have focused our recommendations on programs that target these two venues, as shown in the four quadrants of Figure 8.1. These quadrants represent proactive and reactive strategies in leadership and team development programs.

Figure 8.1 Matrix of Options for Organizational and Leader Renewal

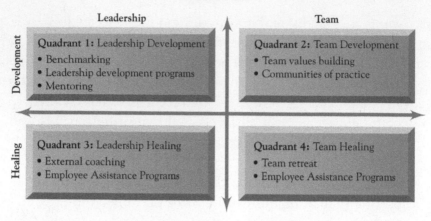

Quadrant 1: Benchmarking

Benchmarking is a process that has been successfully used in many organizations and communities. It is designed to elicit knowledge regarding the best practices around a certain industry or content area. One example of a best practice in the health care industry might be enhanced patient services. An example of benchmarking in a content area might include how social responsibility is enacted across many different industries. Within the context of our discussion on toxicity, benchmarking could be engaged to find the best practices other organizations are using to create concrete, behaviorally specific values related to respectful engagement.

If you determine that benchmarking is a potentially proactive strategy to help leaders understand best practices in a certain area, don't assume the search has to have your industry's focus. We have seen this many times where a nonprofit organization, for example, believes that it has to engage in a best-practice search of how nonprofits handle toxicity. We're not saying that other types of industries must be engaged in the search. However, with our own clients, some of the best practices have emanated from dissimilar industries. For example, one of us worked in a financial services business that benchmarked customer service on an organization that was a far cry from the financial services arena: Disney World! Once you have the best-practices information collected, disseminate it to the team that has an interest in this process, and together you can determine how to incorporate selected actions into the development of your organization.

To get you started on this benchmarking effort, we provide some sample questions you might ask the benchmarked organizations you select to follow. In these, we have focused on questions that relate to the development of values related to respectful engagement and toxic behaviors:

- How have you engaged your organization in practicing your core values on a daily basis?
- How did you determine these core values?
- How have you integrated your values into other core methods: performance appraisal, 360-degree feedback, or strategic planning, for example?
- How have you addressed toxic behaviors with people who do not live up to the values of respectful engagement?
- When a toxic person has violated core values and caused considerable damage in the team, what have you done? Were the values useful in this process? If so, how? If not, why?
- Is toxicity an issue in your organization? Why? Why not?

Quadrant 1: Leadership Development Program

Leadership development programs are an excellent way to educate leaders in strategies for preventing toxicity and fostering respectful engagement. All too often, formal leadership development programs focus on strategic planning, performance management, career development, and negotiations. These are important and needed. However, these programs could become even more valuable if they incorporated the significant building block of values clarification. For example, think about these questions in relation to your organization:

- Are organizational values discussed in these programs?
- Is there a training program on integrating values into your organization's performance appraisal systems?
- Do leaders learn to reinforce organizational values, especially respectful engagement, at the individual and team levels?

In addition, scout around your organization and search for training programs that teach leaders how to deal with toxicity. With a problem this costly in terms of human and financial resources, we're surprised that such programs are practically nonexistent. By including education on toxic systems in existing programs, you have a head start on developing leaders who are alert to the first signs of toxic fire and douse it before there is a raging blaze.

Recently we found that many organizations are initiating programs to cope with "difficult people" largely related to the more blatant bullying behavior. As designers and facilitators of professional development programs that enhance the livability of workplace environments, we are also focusing on the less apparent and more insidious impact of passive aggression and team sabotage. Our clients have confirmed our belief that the elephant in the room is actually the passive hostility that runs rampant throughout teams, undercutting productivity and well-being. One of our clients recently engaged us in a large-scale strategic planning and leadership development endeavor designed exclusively around getting the elephant out in the open. We are receiving reports from other clients that a thorough systemic set of interventions can effectively draw leaders' attention to the significance of the problem in front of them and help them contain the potential harm.

Quadrant 1: Mentoring for Leadership

Research findings on leaders have shown that mentoring programs can contribute to the transformation of leadership qualities within an organization and seed the honoring of values related to respectful engagement.[1] In the next few paragraphs, we show that mentoring can make a contribution to the prevention, or at least the reduction, of toxicity in the workplace.

In a recent ranking of the top one hundred U.S. organizations that excel in human capital development, 77 percent of these companies have formal mentoring programs.[2] Many firms either establish structured mentoring programs or simply encourage managers to create informal mentoring relationships as an additional tool for succession planning, making sure that future leaders are prepared to pick up the reins when others step down. Mentoring programs provide an opportunity not only to grow from within, but also to keep knowledge within the company by increasing retention of leaders. Mentoring has benefited both leaders and organizations by focusing on knowledge transfer, succession planning, and networking. These are significant goals; however, we are suggesting that mentoring has the potential to be much more than the passing on of skills and the advancement of budding protégés.

Mentoring can make a significant contribution to transforming organizational culture.[3] One researcher noted that "the culture of the organization is a reflection of the consciousness of its leaders."[4] Consider the importance of this statement with respect to toxic leaders. An organization that allows a toxic leader to stay in place is making a statement that this type of behavior, sometimes at the highest levels, is tolerable. If instead the leadership creates values that include zero tolerance for toxicity, then a respectful culture can follow.

Mentoring as a one-on-one developmental relationship offers a substantial opportunity to seed not only the value of respectful engagement, but to embrace this value in the mentoring relationship itself. In other words, mentoring relationships are built to engage the leader in thoughtful reflection, honest and direct feedback, obtainable and behaviorally specific professional goals, and fair reward structures. Some organizations take mentoring very seriously and have learning programs to prepare mentors. This is a prime opportunity to make respectful engagement one of the criteria. Mentors not only informally teach critical content areas, but they are preparing prodigies to be socially responsible. Research has found that learning through mentoring has the potential to transform leadership behaviors.[5]

Mentoring relationships create the opportunity to expand a person's understanding of self as engaged with others. Being in a mentoring relationship demands awareness of self and others to facilitate the learning environment. Toxicity has no place in such a relationship and can be confronted directly for the purposes of learning rather than punishment. These teaching moments are the embodiment of "in situ" learning for building constructive workplace relationships. These values and skills can now be brought to group processes, customer relations, and policy design of the organization. A report from one of the leaders in our study reflects the power of a long-term mentoring relationship:

> The mentoring comes up again as a way of preventing this toxicity from taking hold. I let the team know that I've mentored my folks and these problems [disrespectful behavior] do not occur because I am being very proactive by discussing and modeling guidelines for behavior. It [mentoring] is a proactive strategy where I can observe reactions and behaviors and have checkpoints for progress as it relates to our values among other things.

Because mentoring is an important tool in cultural transformation, it has the potential to change the culture of an organization or team from toxic to healthy and at the same time focus on productivity and individual growth. Leaders then ultimately become ambassadors as they engage in teams and one-on-one relationships upholding the values of respect and zero tolerance for toxicity. An executive from our in-depth interviews made a poignant observation about the values of promoting from within in relation to toxic personalities:

> Rarely do we have someone who has grown up in the system, who has these toxic behaviors because we mold our culture so strong, you self-select out at earlier levels. You don't make it ten years here and have those kind of tendencies. There's just no way.
>
> So where we find the biggest adjustment is when we hire high talent, strong performers from outside the industry, with strong degrees, good working experience. A lot of these people have worked for the major consulting firms and they have big egos and a lot of accomplishments, and they're very good at what they do, but they also have very strong personalities. And if those individuals don't recognize how important it is to work within our culture, those are the ones who self-destruct. This toxic person is not from the internal group. And this toxic person was an outside hire who came to the company about twelve years ago.

Quadrant 2: Communities of Practice and Values Building

In this section, we focus on communities of practice as a strategy for building team cohesiveness and values of team collaboration. Another important approach to team building is the team values approach. The values model, described in Chapter Six, is a deliberate and focused program for identifying and maintaining organizational values and team norms consistent with these values. Communities of practice represent a more organic, grassroots initiative that encourages groups to self-organize around common values and interests. According to the originators of the concept of communities of practice in organizational work, "A community of practice is a group of people informally bound together by shared expertise and passion for a joint enterprise."[6] Communities of practice are formed for any number of purposes, including to maintain peer associations when the company reorganizes, respond to large-scale changes, or address new challenges when the organization changes strategy. No matter the circumstances that provide cause for communities of practice to initiate, their members share knowledge in free-flowing and creative ways that encourage new approaches to problems.

Communities of practice relate to toxic personalities as a proactive team strategy—not within a formal team, but ad hoc groups that form to satisfy a passion around a particular area of interest. A leader may wish to form an informal group in the organization to determine how to best drive organizational values into teamwork. Or the leader may put a call to the organization for volunteers to help benchmark how selected organizations that have concrete values deal with toxicity. In spite of the interest, passion, and sustainability of these groups, they are also vulnerable to remaining insular from other ongoing teams. This often happens because the informality of forming and maintaining the group can result in a lack of legitimacy in formal communication and decision-making routes of the organization. Although the very strength of communities of practice is the informality and "off-line" freedom of the exchange, the learning and discoveries of the group are often relevant to ongoing issues being handled more formally.

In our experience, the innovative contributions of the community of practice are sometimes lost because there is no formal communication channel to leadership. For this reason, we suggest that leaders find ways to access and be open to the ideas that emerge from these informal groups. The content of what has been discovered can be subject to further and formal analysis, integrated within the context of strategic problem solving, or even within small- and large-group discussions in formal leadership development. In relating communities of practice to toxic personality work, the passion of the group would be around respectful engagement. Perhaps the initial reason is that members of the practice are suffering bouts with a toxic person. Perhaps team members have an overall interest in integrity, social responsibility, and honest communication with a direct focus on respectful engagement.

As a proactive strategy, healthy, energized communities of practice help prevent toxicity from flourishing in the organization. As we have said many times in this book, involvement catalyzes better commitment, ownership, and results. Following are some of the criteria that leaders need to engage to bring about the successful communities of practice:

- Meetings should be scheduled at regular intervals.
- There need to be focused discussions that are open to innovative ideas and process events.
- A facilitator is often chosen from the group to keep the discussions on track.
- Each meeting has an agenda developed by the group.
- The community of practice formally shares the results of its actions as determined by group consensus.
- Use virtual technology to keep those who have not been able to attend a meeting informed.
- Use virtual meeting technology to keep the face-to-face time to a minimum such that geographically dispersed members may participate.
- Consider challenges across the organization, not just within a small team.

Schedule Meetings Regularly. Although they are informal, meetings should be regularly scheduled. For example, everyone knows that at noon on Fridays, a one-hour community of practice is scheduled in a certain area that crosses organizational boundaries or needs.

Focus the Discussion, Use a Facilitator, and Set an Agenda. The group members facilitating keep the meeting on track, record results, give everyone who wishes to speak an opportunity to be heard, and in general coordinate the meeting so that the free flow of ideas is effectively managed and processed. Attention to the group process and the focus of the group are important in keeping the group energized and involved. There's an agenda for each meeting, determined by the group, that keeps the group focused and moving forward toward their goals.

Share the Results. The trickiest part of communities of practice is to search for a formal way to report results and potential actions taken. One of the best ways to initiate this is to ask members to identify someone they know and trust who would lend legitimacy to what they are doing. They could ask these individuals to attend a community of practice meeting, a member could send a report to these individuals, or members could schedule meetings with these key persons to provide a context for their work and how they need the help of these others to move their agenda into the organization.

Use Virtual Technology. Virtual technology can be used to share the agenda and report results. Between meetings, online community-building software could be used to prepare for the face-to-face meetings as well as to keep everyone involved and communicating between meetings, particularly for those who have not been able to attend.

Keep in Mind the Organization as a Whole. A community of practice transcends organizational boundaries. It is used for systemwide issues, a perfect venue for values clarification work. As you can see from this process, it's a backdrop for information gathering (from within and outside the organization), brain-storming, problem solving, and action planning. It is an arena where information sharing, social connection, innovative col-laboration, and respectful dialogue can flourish. And when this occurs, organizational renewal has begun, and there is no place for toxic behaviors.

Quadrant 3: External Coaching for Leadership Healing and Employee Assistance Programs

In Chapter Seven, we discussed engaging a coach to help a toxic person realize new behaviors that are aligned with the values of the organization. In this chapter, we reintroduce coaching from a different context: helping a leader deal with the aftermath of emotional injury caused by a toxic individual.

The leader must first discern if coaching is the best choice for professional help. In some cases, leaders may need to seek the assistance of a psychologist (perhaps through the Employee Assistance Program, EAP) who can guide them back to a sense of well-being. Many of our leaders in the survey reported seeing mental health counselors to help them cope with a toxic person at work. Some of the leaders ended up in the hospital as their physical health deteriorated so severely from the daily toll of toxicity from their boss, as this senior vice president related to us:

> Working under my toxic leader, I never realized the toll this had taken on my health and well-being until I found myself in a hospital bed at age forty, having just had a heart attack. As I reflected, I had done so much to try and make this leader successful that in the end, I had put not only my career, reputation, and family at risk, but also my life. At the time, it had seemed so right. If only I could compensate for his weaknesses.... That was what I was there for. Then I felt if only I worked harder, longer, smarter—then it moves from they are failing to you are failing.

How should the leader best engage a coach? There is no formula that answers this question in all circumstances. However, critical to choosing the right coach is the coach's area of expertise as relevant to the leader's learning needs and fit in terms of how comfortable a leader feels in sharing significant information with the coach.

We believe that the coach should not be anyone within the organization. Rather, we have found with our own clients that they are typically much more comfortable with someone from outside the organization. Likely, they want and need the objectivity of someone outside the system to freely express their experiences of anger, frustration, and injury in working with the toxic person.

To discern the appropriateness of a coach in helping a leader deal with the aftermath of the toxic individual, here are some sample questions to ask prospective coaches:

- Are you a certified coach?
- What is your specialty area?
- What are your experiences in working with leaders who have had to deal with a toxic person?
- What is your understanding of toxic behaviors in the workplace and how they affect those around them?
- What are some results I may expect?

When choosing a coach for healing in the wake of toxicity, ensure that the coach understands the broad spectrum of symptoms that can be triggered in people who are enduring toxic behaviors daily.

Quadrant 4: Team Healing Through Retreats and Employee Assistance Programs

The effects of a toxic person are not restricted to one target person. In most cases, the toxic person's entire team suffers greatly. Whether the toxic person is still within the organization or has left, programs for healing the team are advised. Although both contexts present challenges for the leader, the situation is more difficult if the toxic individual is still in the organization.

If the toxic individual remains within the organization, team members who want to express their frustration, anger, and concern with his or her toxic behaviors often approach a leader.

Leaders need to be careful neither to breach the privacy of the toxic person with confidential information they may hold nor denigrate the toxic person in spite of their own frustration with him or her. Nor should the leader simply hand out advice about how to deal with the person; instead, the leader needs to listen carefully to the complaint, acknowledge the team member's concerns, and suggest seeking help through the Employee Assistance Program (EAP) within or outside the organization. EAPs have a broad array of resources, including professional counseling services. Leaders should not put themselves in a situation where they become the de facto sounding board or pseudotherapist to the person in need of healing. Professionals trained in dealing with mental health concerns are better prepared to handle these situations. Likewise, the leader should not neglect his or her own emotional needs and should consider help through EAP providers.

If the toxic person is no longer within the organization, the leader may still recommend the EAP route, especially for those who have been targeted by the toxic person or appear to be having significant difficulty getting back on track even after the toxic person has left.

Concurrently, the leader could initiate a team retreat facilitated by an external consultant. Organization development consultants are well equipped to help leaders design a strategy that will address the typical emotional aftermath of team toxicity. In general, teams need a period for relating their suffering, but the focus is on healing, not complaining. It is critical that teams are not permitted to simply engage in bad-mouthing the toxic person.

Instead, we suggest an approach that is affirming and looks to the future. Remember that much of the team's energy has been devoted to avoiding, going around others, withdrawing, or complaining about the toxic team member. Although many may have left the organization rather than endure this situation, those who remain have found solace in a common "enemy." They need to rediscover an esprit de corps that is based on positive, productive energy. The following key questions could be explored in this team development retreat:

- Does our organization or team have the stated values that reinforce operating in ways that respect the dignity of each employee and external stakeholder?
- If not, what do we need to do to engage this? If we do, what are the next steps for us?
- What are some obstacles that prevent us from achieving the respect and dignity we all need?
- What should we do about these obstacles?

In scheduling these interventions, we have discovered there needs to be follow-up with the team; don't succumb to a onetime event. If your funds are limited, the better choice is to have two shorter sessions separated by some work by the team in between rather than one longer session.

Finally, a little goes a long way here: select just one or two core actions that the team will take. Keep in mind that the first priority at this point is to help the team heal and be prepared to work productively.

Along with this, we suggest identifying both team actions and individual actions. In working with teams that are recovering from toxicity, we have found that the best ways to change how the team relates and moves forward to healthier relationships depend on these actions: each individual in the group should make a commitment and reaffirmation to the values of direct communication, individuals should not go behind anyone's back, and individuals should not gossip about the toxic person who has left.

Our Final Words

Of all the consulting arenas in which we have worked, dealing with toxicity is probably one of the most difficult for clients. Nevertheless, based on our own research, the research of others, and our practice experiences, we believe that toxic behaviors and the ensuing toxic relationships can be changed with a systems approach. Using this method, the leader can rise above blaming the toxic person and use the opportunity to create living organizational values that will change the way people in the organization work together through respectful engagement.

The TOCS approach is about respectful engagement with individuals and the organization. Being a leader is about integrity, authenticity, and social responsibility:

- Integrity is about a leader's consistency in standing up for the values he or she believes in.
- Authenticity is about leaders walking their own talk, modeling the core values in actions on a daily basis.
- Social responsibility is being good organizational citizens by respecting individuals within the organization and key stakeholders outside it.

When all three contexts are lived to the fullest, leaders have the capacity to deal with toxicity in the most effective, systemic way possible.

We hope this book has lived up to your expectations in providing you with truly values-driven approaches that are systemic in nature and make your organizations more humane and productive through respectful engagement.

Appendix A

OUR RESEARCH METHODOLOGY

In our study, we were interested in leaders' experiences working with toxic persons. We used a mixed-method design—a research approach that employs both qualitative and quantitative design and analysis. The qualitative portion of our study used a grounded theory design. *Grounded theory* is a research method that allows the researcher to understand the experience a person has of the chosen phenomenon and the meaning that he or she attaches to that experience. The quantitative portion of the study included a survey questionnaire that was distributed to a sample of leaders in the United States.

The study unfolded in three phases. The findings from phase 1 contributed to our development of the interview approach and structure; in phase 2, the in-depth interview findings were used to inform the development and design of phase 3, the survey portion. All findings from these three phases are reflected in our conceptualization of the TOCS model.

Phase 1: Informal Interviews

We informally interviewed fifty "thought leaders" without any structured questions. We call these individuals "thought leaders" because they were selected based on being reflective in understanding problems from multiple viewpoints. These were simply good, all-around leaders who were respected in their fields and were regarded for their management abilities.

These leaders were not selected because we knew they worked with toxic individuals. Rather, we simply wanted to ask a general population if they had experiences with toxic personalities and, if so, what that was like. Our goal was to determine if we were on the right track regarding the power and negative effects of toxic personalities at work. We didn't even have a formulated definition of *toxic personality* at this point. What was surprising to us is that we found out we didn't need a precise definition: every leader knew what we were talking about. We simply said "toxic personality," and they launched into stories of their suffering. Interesting to us, there appeared almost a cathartic effect that occurred with their reliving the experience and talking with someone who could name this phenomenon. Numerous times, they commented on a sense of validation that they were perhaps not alone in experiencing this situation in spite of the fact that it had never been addressed in their management forums.

We discovered that each one of these thought leaders has worked with or did work with a toxic individual. Tapping their minds on how they may have parlayed some of their successes with the toxic individual, we had no preset agenda of interview questions. We simply had informal conversations with them about their experiences in working with toxic individuals.

Interestingly, toxicity and its repercussions were never talked about in any leadership training they attended, the coaching sessions they participated in, or any team-building programs. Although they touted the use of performance management mechanisms with these toxic personalities, some saw these strategies as only mildly successful and others not at all. These informal conversations revealed that toxic workplaces were common, the human suffering and lost productivity in dealing with toxic persons were significant, and there were no systematic programs for managing toxicity in their workplaces.

At this point, we determined that it would be useful and feasible to study toxic situations through the eyes of the leader to uncover the meaning and effects of this commonly recognized, but often ignored, workplace problem.

Phase 2: Formal Interviews

The second phase of the study was qualitative and consisted of unstructured hour-long interviews with leaders of profit and nonprofit organizations. These successful leaders held positions including CEO/executive, director, manager, supervisor, project manager, and team leader of both Fortune 500 companies and nonprofit health care organizations.

We did not determine at first the precise number of leaders we would interview. Instead, we used a grounded theory approach: we continued interviewing until we kept hearing repetitions and, subsequently, could formulate a theory "grounded" in what we were hearing. We reached this theoretical saturation point of repetitious findings in just fifteen interviews.

All interviews (which produced more than three hundred pages of transcripts) were recorded, transcribed, and coded. The codes used to describe the experiences being related to us were taken directly from the participants' own words. We continued to interview and code until we no longer found any new information from the interviewees. In most of these interviews, it was apparent that our interviewees had had several encounters dealing with these toxic situations and could still vividly describe their experience even thirty years later.

Using the leaders' stories and experiences, we built a conceptual understanding of the significant issues that were meaningful to the toxic situation in the workplace. From more than a hundred descriptive codes, we came up with five primary areas of importance to the toxic situation:

• The toxic person's characteristics and behaviors
• The leader's reactions to the toxic person
• The leader's strategies for dealing with the toxic person
• The effects of toxicity on the system
• The role of organizational culture on toxicity

Each of these five areas was described and illustrated over and over again by interviewees' stories of toxicity in the workplace.

Phase 3: The Structured Survey

The third phase of our mixed-method design was the development of a structured survey created from the interviews that we had conducted and analyzed in phase 2 of the study. The purpose of the survey was to determine the relevance or generalizability of our interview findings to a larger sample of leaders and refine our understanding of the toxic situation.

We designed a survey with eighty-two items that included demographic information, a ratings scale, and opportunities to comment on a specific item. All questions were developed from the five primary themes identified in the interview analysis, including the language that our interviewees used around these themes. The survey was distributed to 962 potential respondents who were employed in large, medium, and small profit and non-profit organizations in the United States. We had a return rate of 42 percent (404 completed surveys). We used these data to calculate the descriptive statistics or percentages attached to each item.

Next we conducted an exploratory factor analysis to determine which items were the most robust in describing each of the five primary areas: toxic behaviors, leader reactions, leader strategies, system effects, and organizational culture. The results of the factor analyses yielded four factors of interest:

- Toxic behaviors
- Leader reactions
- Leader strategies
- Organizational culture

In relationship to the five areas in the qualitative analysis, all five were confirmed, but "organizational system" and "culture" were collapsed into one factor with two separate areas within: "system effects" and "organizational values." Each factor had two or three components. For example, "Factor 1: Toxic Behaviors" was made up of three areas: shaming, passive hostility, and team sabotage. Each factor and its respective components are described fully in the text with figures to assist in understanding the richness of these significant characteristics of toxicity in the workplace.

Once we had completed the factor analysis, we employed inferential statistics to examine the effect of demographic and leadership characteristics in relation to toxic behaviors, leader reactions, leader strategies, and organizational culture. We were interested in the following information:

- The relationship of profit or nonprofit organizational status
- The gender of the toxic person
- The gender of the leader
- The degree of toxicity
- The organizational relationship between the toxic person and the leader to the four factors

The findings from the inferential analyses are presented throughout the book; these are specifically relevant in determining the effectiveness of leader strategies associated with their organizational power relative to the toxic person.

The survey was designed to invite respondents to add their own comments in relationship to the topics of toxic behaviors, their reactions, strategies they have used, and the effects of toxicity on teams and organizational culture. We received seventy-two pages of single-spaced comments. These comments were vivid depictions of people's experiences and reflections on this topic. We have shared many of these comments in this book to convey the poignancy and earnestness that our respondents brought to this study—a level of response and presence for which we are deeply grateful.

Appendix B

NATIONAL SURVEY RESPONSES ON TOXIC BEHAVIORS

Toxic Behaviors: Survey Responses to Exhibit 2.1

In this section, you will plot your responses to the questions in Exhibit 2.1, which will reflect the behaviors that describe the toxic person with whom you have worked. The number of each item in Table B.1 corresponds to the questions listed in Exhibit 2.1. Each of these items contributed to the three types of toxic behaviors discussed in Chapter Two: shaming, passive hostility, and team sabotage. We have indicated what group the item belongs to based on our analysis of the survey responses in Table B.2. Only the items from the survey that were significantly related to one another within each of the three groups have been included.

You can compare your answers from Exhibit 2.1 to the survey participants' responses. To show you how it works, take the first item, "Humiliates others." Just as in Exhibit 2.1, the respondents were given six choices to describe the toxic person they had worked with or were currently working with. The top three items—"Yes, definitely characteristic of this person," "Mostly characteristic of this person," and "Somewhat characteristic of this person"—were considered a high to moderate endorsement, respectively, that the toxic person did humiliate others. Similarly, we considered the bottom three descriptions—"A little characteristic of this person," "Very little characteristic of this person," and "Definitely not at all characteristic of this person"—as indications that the toxic behavior of "humiliates others" was not frequently or not at all a behavior that the toxic person exhibited.

Table B.1 shows you the percentage of all respondents, who answered the question, that checked that response. Thus, in item 1, 24 percent of respondents indicated that "humiliates others" was definitely characteristic of the person that they considered toxic. If we add up the percentages of the top three responses, then we have 69 percent of respondents endorsed "humiliates others" as a toxic behavior that they had experienced. Now compare your responses from Exhibit 2.1 to the percentage of responses that agreed with you. If you answered item 1 as "somewhat characteristic of this person," then 26 percent of the respondents in our survey agreed with you.

Here is a final step you might take if you want to discover which type of toxic behaviors—shaming, passive hostility, or team sabotage—the person you are thinking of is most likely to use. To help you recognize which survey items pertain to each of these three behaviors, we have shaded the corresponding areas: shaming items are depicted as the lightest shaded area, passive hostility as the next lightest, and team sabotage as the darkest (Table B.2). We have completed an example by filling in hypothetical scores for each item, so you can see just how it works. First, insert the number in the appropriate column that corresponds with your response choice (not at all characteristic, very little characteristic, little characteristic, somewhat characteristic, mostly characteristic, definitely characteristic). Second, add up the column scores and place them in the appropriate "total scores" row. Third, divide by the number of scores in the column. Take the average of your score as indicated on the table chart and enter it into the graph in Figure B.1. Now you can see the profile of the type of behaviors that are driving you to distraction! It could be that you endorsed

Table B.1 Toxic Behaviors: Distribution of Survey Responses

ITEMS FROM SURVEY	NOT CHARACTERISTIC			CHARACTERISTIC		
	Definitely not at all characteristic of this person	Very little characteristic of this person	A little characteristic of this person	Somewhat characteristic of this person	Mostly characteristic of this person	Definitely characteristic of this person
	1	2	3	4	5	6
1. Humiliates others	6%	10%	15%	26%	19%	24%
2. Uses sarcastic remarks	3	4	9	17	26	42
3. Takes potshots	3	6	9	19	29	35
4. Distrusts opinions of others	2	1	4	17	25	52
5. Monitors team behaviors to point of surveillance	4	9	11	21	20	35
6. Meddles in teamwork	3	6	9	26	32	25
7. Uses authority to punish others	6	8	11	17	22	37
8. Demonstrates passive-aggressive behaviors	2	3	5	9	24	57
9. Protects one's own territory	1	2	2	7	29	69
10. Has difficulty accepting negative feedback	1	4	3	14	23	56
11. Is clueless that they are toxic to others	2	3	4	7	32	52
12. Points out the mistakes of others	0	2	3	10	34	51

Table B.2 Items That Contribute to Three Types of Toxic Behaviors

	SHAMING	PASSIVE HOSTILITY	TEAM SABOTAGE
1. Humiliates others	3		
2. Sarcastic remarks	3		
3. Potshots	3		
4. Distrusts opinions of others		4	
5. Monitors team behaviors			5
6. Meddles in teamwork			6
7. Uses authority to punish others			6
8. Passive aggressive		6	
9. Protects own territory		4	
10. Difficulty accepting feedback		5	
11. Clueless that they are toxic		5	
12. Points out the mistakes of others	1		
TOTAL SCORES	Add up all scores in column (10)	Add up all scores in column (24)	Add up all scores in column (17)
AVERAGE SCORE	Divide by 4 (2.5)	Divide by 5 (4.8)	Divide by 3 (5.6)

them all at a high level, and it would not be unusual if you did. However, you may find that one type of behavior predominates over the others and increases your awareness of what changes need to be targeted. In the example, the toxic person excels in passive hostility and team sabotage behaviors.

Figure B.1 Plotting the Toxic Behaviors

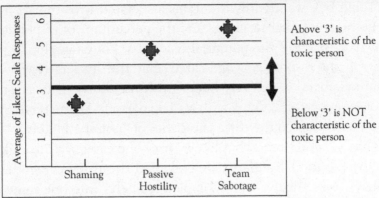

Leader Reactions: Survey Responses to Exhibit 3.1

In Table B.3, we identify the items associated with the six most predominant leader reactions and the percentage of respondents that rated each of the potential reactions. For example, 20 percent of our respondents indicated that the leaders (including team members) were "very likely" to leave their organization as a consequence of working with a toxic person. As the table indicates, we collapsed the three categories of "not at all likely," "not too likely," and "somewhat likely" into one category: "not likely leader reaction." Similarly, we collapsed the three categories of "likely," "very likely," and "completely likely" into one category: "likely leader reaction." On the first item, the cumulative percentage for those who indicated it was likely their reaction to leave their organization is 51 percent (14% likely + 20% very likely + 17% completely likely).

Table B.4 shows the two primary types of leader reactions to toxic personalities identified from our research study: the leader adjusts or leaves (lighter shaded area) or the leader reconfigures the situation (darker shaded area). Each survey item in this table pertains to one of these two reactions.

The instructions given in the first section of this appendix will help you complete this table. Briefly, insert the number in the appropriate category that corresponds with your response choice (not at all likely, not too likely, somewhat likely, likely, very likely, completely likely). Then add the column scores and place them in the corresponding "total scores" row. Finally, divide by the number of items identified in that category and put in the average score row. You can now plot your scores on Figure B.2 and see if your typical reactions are in one cluster of behaviors or the other or both.

Table B.3 Leader Reactions: Distribution of Survey Responses

ITEMS FROM SURVEY	Not at all likely	Not too likely	Somewhat Likely	Likely	Very likely	Completely likely
	1	2	3	4	5	6
	NOT LIKELY LEADER REACTION			LIKELY LEADER REACTION		
1. Leave the organization	5%	18%	26%	14%	20%	17%
2. Accommodate the toxic person	1	4	19	29	33	13
3. Compromise their standards	4	16	22	24	26	7
4. Reduce interactions with the toxic person	1	4	9	12	33	41
5. Exclude the toxic person from important decisions	8	23	13	19	16	22
6. Take responsibilities away from the toxic person	17	34	13	15	11	11

Table B.4 Two Types of Leader Reactions to Toxic Behaviors

	ADJUST OR LEAVE	RECONFIGURE THE SITUATION
1. Leave the organization		
2. Accommodate the toxic person		
3. Compromise their standards		
4. Reduce interactions with toxic person		
5. Exclude toxic person from important decisions		
6. Take responsibilities away from the toxic person		
7. Decrease their motivation		
TOTAL SCORES	Add up all scores in column	Add up all scores in column
AVERAGE SCORE	Divide by 4	Divide by 3

Figure B.2 Plotting the Leader Reaction Scores

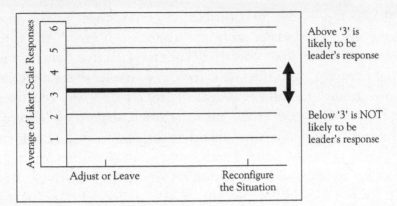

Leader Strategies: Survey Responses to Exhibit 3.2

Table B.5 provides the distribution of responses to the most significant items related to leader strategies. It groups the three responses of "not at all effective," "not too effective," and "somewhat effective" into the one category of "ineffective strategies." It also groups the three responses of "effective," "very effective," and "completely effective" into the one category of "effective strategies." Notice in this table that the majority of cumulative response rates are under "ineffective strategies." For example, item 2, "Talking with the person regarding the negative behavior," was rated by 94 percent of the respondents under the "ineffective strategy" group.

Table B.6 identifies the three types of strategies leaders use to deal with toxic personalities. The items pertaining to these three categories are correspondingly shaded (formal strategies in the lightest shade, informal strategies in the darker shade, and feedback strategies in the darkest shade). The instructions given in the first section of this appendix will help you complete this table. To summarize these instructions, insert the number in the category that corresponds to your response choice (not at all effective, not too effective, somewhat effective, effective, very effective, completely effective). Second, add the column scores and place them in the "total scores" row. Third, divide by the number identified in the average score row. Now you can examine what group of strategies you tend to use when working with the toxic person. See Figure B.3.

Table B.5 Leader Strategies: Distribution of Survey Responses

ITEMS IN SURVEY	Not At All Effective 1	Not Too Effective 2	Somewhat Effective 3	Effective 4	Very Effective 5	Completely Effective 6
	INEFFECTIVE STRATEGIES			EFFECTIVE STRATEGIES		
1. Communicating clear standards to the toxic person	17%	33%	32%	12%	5%	1%
2. Talking with the person regarding the negative behavior	30	34	30	3	4	0
3. Discussing with the person how his or her career may be affected by his or her behavior	34	33	24	7	3	0
4. Avoiding confrontation with the toxic person	16	33	29	13	7	2
5. Communicating to the person how his or her behavior violates organizational values	21	41	27	7	3	0
6. Sticking to my own agenda in spite of the toxic person's particular agenda	7	18	34	26	11	4
7. Engaging in damage control by cleaning up after them for messes they have created in the work lives of others	14	31	33	18	3	1
8. Consulting with someone who has a high degree of integrity within the organization on how to deal with the individual	8	23	29	20	13	5
9. Bringing in an external consultant	30	34	20	10	5	1
10. Documenting and then working to get the person fired	32	22	19	14	6	7
11. Bringing in a team of professionals to confront the toxic person	28	27	24	12	5	4
12. Giving the toxic person performance feedback	21	31	32	8	6	1
13. Managing the negative impact of the toxic person on my own work	5	18	42	23	11	1

Table B.6 Three Types of Leader Strategies

	FORMAL STRATEGIES	INFORMAL STRATEGIES	FEEDBACK STRATEGIES
1. Relating clear standards of behavior you will not tolerate			
2. Relating the negative effects the toxic person has on others			
3. Discussing the effect on the toxic person's career			
4. Avoiding confrontation with the toxic person			
5. Relating how his/her behavior violates organizational values			
6. Sticking to my own agenda			
7. Engaging in damage control			
8. Consulting with a trusted person within the organization			
9. Bringing in an external consultant			
10. Documenting and then working to get the person fired			
11. Bringing in a team of professionals to confront the toxic person			
12. Giving the toxic person performance feedback			
13. Managing the negative impact of the toxic person on my own work			
TOTAL SCORES	Add up all scores in column	Add up all scores in column	Add up all scores in column
AVERAGE SCORE	Divide by 3	Divide by 5	Divide by 5

Figure B.3 Plotting Leader Strategies Scores

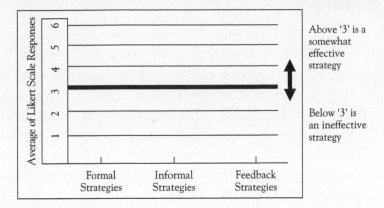

Organizational Culture: Survey Responses to Exhibit 4.1

We provide the distribution of percentage responses to the items associated with organizational culture in Table B.7. The responses from each of three categories have been collapsed into two primary categories ("disagree") and ("agree"). In this table, note that items 1 and 6 refer to the organizational culture having strong values that provided significant guidelines to eradicate toxic behaviors and that the majority of the respondents fell in the "disagree" group. In the remaining items, the majority of respondents fell into the "agree" group in describing the detrimental system effects of toxic behaviors.

Table B.8 identifies the two types of organizational responses to the toxic person—system reactions and organizational values. The two shaded areas correspond to one of these organizational responses (the lighter shading is associated with system reactions, the darker area to organizational values). The first part of this appendix provides detailed instructions for you to complete this portion of the table. Briefly, insert the number associated with the item that corresponds with your response (strongly disagree, disagree, somewhat disagree, somewhat agree, agree, and strongly agree). Second, add the column numbers and place in the "total scores" row. Third, divide by the number of items in the category to get your average score. Now plot it on the graph in Figure B.4 to characterize your organizational culture around system reactions and organizational values.

Table B.7 Organizational Culture: Distribution of Survey Responses

ITEMS FROM SURVEY	Strongly Disagree	Disagree	Somewhat Disagree	Somewhat Agree	Agree	Strongly Agree
	1	2	3	4	5	6
		DISAGREE			AGREE	
1. The organizational values provide concrete behaviors in how we deal with the toxic person	13%	30%	19%	23%	13%	2%
2. The climate changes when the toxic person is present	1	0	0	13	29	58
3. The structure of the organization changes to accommodate the toxic person's behavior	6	17	15	29	26	7
4. It takes a long time for the toxic person's behavior to come to the attention of the leaders	7	13	12	20	26	22
5. The organizational environment contributed to the toxic person's getting away with counterproductive behavior	4	8	4	23	36	25
6. The organizational culture has a low tolerance for toxic behavior	14	37	21	16	9	3
7. The organization tolerates toxicity if the person is productive	2	7	8	31	35	17
8. Team meetings are less productive	0	4	6	22	36	32

Table B.8 Two Types of Organizational Culture Responses

	SYSTEM REACTIONS	ORGANIZATIONAL VALUES
1. The organizational values provide concrete behaviors to deal with the toxic person		
2. The climate changes when the toxic person is present		
3. The structure of the organization changes to accommodate the toxic person		
4. It takes a long time for the toxic person's behavior to be noticed by the leaders		
5. The organizational environment contributes to the toxic person getting away with the behavior		
6. The organizational culture has a low tolerance for toxic behavior		
7. The organization tolerates toxicity if the person is productive		
8. Team meetings are less productive		
TOTAL SCORES	Add up all scores in column	Add up all scores in column
AVERAGE SCORE	Divide by 6	Divide by 2

Figure B.4 Plotting System Reactions and Organizational Values

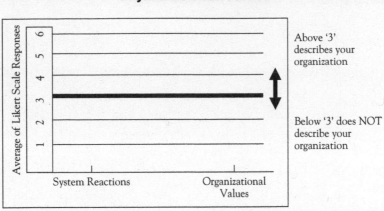

Notes

Chapter One

1. Keashley, L., & Jagatic, K. (2000, August). *The nature, extent, and impact of emotional abuse in the workplace: Results of a statewide survey.* Paper presented at the Academy of Management Conference, Toronto, Canada.
2. Solfield, L., & Salmond, S. W. (2003). Workplace violence. *Orthopaedic Nursing, 22*(4), 274–283.
3. Miner, A. G., Glomb, T. M., & Hulin, C. (2005). Experience sampling mood and its correlates at work. *Journal of Occupational and Organizational Psychology, 78,* 171–193.
4. Sutton, R. (2007). Building the civilized workplace. *McKinsey Quarterly, 2,* 47–55.
5. Barrick, M. R., Stewart, G. L., Neubert, M. J., & Mount, M. K. (1998). Relating member ability and personality to work-team processes and team effectiveness. *Journal of Applied Psychology, 83*(3), 377–391.
6. Lepine, J., Hollenbeck, J., Ilgen, D., & Hedlund, J. (1997). Effects of individual differences on the performance of hierarchical decision-making teams: Much more than g. *Journal of Applied Psychology, 82*(5), 803–811.
7. Pearson, C. M., & Porath, C. L. (2005). On the nature, consequences and remedies of workplace incivility: No time for "nice"? Think again. *Academy of Management Executive, 19*(1), 7–19.
8. Pearson, C. M., Andersson, L. M., & Porath, C. L. (2000). Assessing and attacking workplace incivility. *Organizational Dynamics, 29*(2), 123–137.
9. Pearson and Porath. (2005).
10. Ferris, G. R., Zinko, R., Brouer, R. L., Buckely, M. R., & Harvey, M. G. (2007). Strategic bullying as a supplementary, balanced perspective on destructive leadership. *Leadership Quarterly, 18,* 195–206.
11. Tepper, B. J. (2000). Consequences of abusive supervision. *Academy of Management Journal, 43*(2), 178–190.
12. Hodson, R., Roscigno, V. J., & Lopez, S. H. (2006). Chaos and the abuse of power: Workplace bullying in organizational and interactional context. *Work and Occupations, 33*(4), 382–416.

13. Neuman, G. A., & Wright, J. (1999). Team effectiveness: Beyond skills and cognitive ability. *Journal of Applied Psychology, 84*(3), 376–389.
14. Cascio, W. (2000). *Costing human resources* (4th ed.). Cincinnati, OH: South-Western.
15. Camacho, M. L., & Paulus, P. B. (1995). The role of social anxiousness in group brainstorming. *Journal of Personality and Social Psychology, 68*(6), 1071–1080.
16. Labianca, G., & Brass, D. J. (2006). Exploring the social ledger: Negative relationships and negative asymmetry in social networks in organizations. *Administrative Science Quarterly, 31*(3), 596–614.

Part Two
1. Capra, F. (1996). *The web of life: A new scientific understanding of living systems.* New York: Doubleday.
2. Langan-Fox, J., Cooper, C. L., & Klimoski, R. (Eds.). (2007). *Research companion to the dysfunctional workplace: Management challenges and symptoms.* Northampton, MA: Edward Elgar.

Chapter Five
1. Dutton, J. (2003). *Energize your workplace: How to create and sustain high quality connections at work.* San Francisco: Jossey-Bass.
2. Jacobs, R. W. (1994). *Real time strategic change: How to involve an entire organization in fast and far-reaching change.* San Francisco: Berrett-Koehler.

Chapter Six
1. Barrick, M. R., & Mount, M. K. (1991). The big five personality dimensions and job performance: A meta-analysis. *Personnel Psychology, 44*(1), 1–26.
2. Buckingham, M., & Coffman, C. (1999). *First, break all the rules. What the world's greatest managers do differently.* New York: Simon & Schuster.
3. Watson Wyatt. (2003). *Connecting organizational communication to financial performance.* Washington, DC: Author.
4. *Campbell-Hallam-Team Development Survey.* (1994). Arlington, VA: Vangent.
5. Essex, L., & Kusy, M. (2007). *Manager's desktop consultant: Just-in-time solutions to the top people problems that keep you up at night.* Mountain View, CA: Davies-Black.

Chapter Seven
1. Essex, L., & Kusy, M. (2007). *Manager's desktop consultant: Just-in-time solutions to the top people problems that keep you up at night.* Mountain View, CA: Davies-Black.
2. Lepsinger, R., & Lucia, A. D. (2001). Performance management and decision making. In D. W. Bracken, C. W. Timmreck, & A. H. Church (Eds.), *The handbook of multisource feedback: The comprehensive source for designing and implementing MSF processes* (pp. 318–334). San Francisco: Jossey-Bass.
3. Tornow, W. W., & Tornow, C. P. (2001). Linking multisource feedback content with organizational needs. In D. W. Bracken, C. W. Timmreck, & A. H. Church (Eds.), *The handbook of multisource feedback: The comprehensive source for designing and implementing MSF processes.* (pp. 48–62). San Francisco: Jossey-Bass.
4. Creative Metrics. *Check-up 360.* http://www.creativemetrics.com/checkupSurvey.aspx?id=28.

5. International Coach Federation. (2008). *What is a coach?* Retrieved July 13, 2008, from http://www.coachfederation.org/ICF/For+Current+Members/Member+Resources/Research/Reports.htm.

6. Holloway, E. L. (2007, May 5). *Coaching leaders in times of transformation.* Keynote address to the IAS Institute, Bad Ragaz, Switzerland.

7. Holloway. (2007).

Chapter Eight

1. Godshalk, V. M., & Sosik, J. J. (2000). Does mentor-protégé agreement on mentor leadership behavior influence the quality of a mentoring relationship? *Group and Organization Management, 25,* 291–317.

2. Training Magazine, http://www.trainingmag.com, as quoted by R. A. Carr, Peer Resources Canada, April 14, 2003.

3. Holloway, E. L. (2006, June 15). *Mentoring for transformational change.* Plenary address to the Oxford Mentoring and Coaching Institute Conference, Oxford, England.

4. Barrett, R. (2006). *Building a values-driven organization.* New York: Elsevier, p. 20

5. Scandura, T. A., & Williams, E. A. (2004). Mentoring and transformational leadership: The role of supervisory career mentoring. *Journal of Vocational Behavior, 65,* 448–468.

6. Wenger, E. C., & Snyder, W. M. (2000, January/February). Communities of practice: The organizational frontier. *Harvard Business Review, 78*(1), 139–145.

The Authors

Dr. Mitchell Kusy has twenty-five years of experience as a key leader in several organizations, including as director of leadership development at American Express and director of organization development at Health Partners. A Registered Organization Development Consultant, he is a full professor in the Ph.D. program in Leadership and Change at Antioch University and a distinguished visiting professor at the University of Auckland, New Zealand. A 2005 Fulbright Scholar for international organization development, he also received the Minnesota Organization Development Practitioner of the Year award in 1998. He has published more than one hundred articles and five books, has been a featured guest on talk shows, and has been interviewed by such publications as the *New York Times* and *Fortune*. He consults internationally in organization development, leadership development, and strategic planning.

Dr. Elizabeth Holloway has worked for over twenty-five years with professionals in human services and management in the areas of supervision, coaching, mentoring, and team development. Her systems approach to learning relationships in work settings has been adopted in training institutes in the United Kingdom, Europe, Asia, and the Middle East. A licensed psychologist and Diplomate of Professional Psychology, she is currently a full professor in the Ph.D. program in Leadership and Change at Antioch

University. She has held professorships at the Universities of California, Utah, Oregon, and Wisconsin. She was named Fellow by the American Psychological Association for her contribution to science and the profession of counseling psychology. She has published extensively and spoken throughout the world on her research and practice in professional relationships. Her current consulting and research are in the areas of coaching, mentoring, and toxicity in the workplace.

Index

A

Abuse of authority, 35–36. *See also* team sabotage

Aggression: legal threshold of abuse, 27. *See also* passive hostility

Agreeableness, 116

Authority, 178–179

B

Bad apple syndrome, 18–19

Benchmarking, 194–195

Bullying: hidden costs of, 15

Butterfly effect, 85

C

Campbell-Hallam-Team Development Survey (TDS), 132–135

Cerner, 5–6

Check-up 360, 166

Climate, 74–76

Cluelessness of one's own toxicity, 31–32, 184–185. *See also* passive hostility

Coaches, 64–65

Coaching, 168–169; accountability to the organization, 170–171; assessing information from multiple stakeholders, 171–172; external coaching for leader healing and employee assistance programs, 203–204; knowing when coaching won't work, 172–173; with people who resist change, 170; recommending reassignment of toxic individuals, 173–174; reintegrating the toxic person into a team, 174–175; systems approach to coaching leaders (SACL), 171–172; using a systems approach, 169–170

Coaching up, 59

Cognitive tests, 116

Communities of practice, 199–203

Competence vs. likability, 114, 191–192

Conscientiousness, 116

Consultants, 64–65, 187–188; and exit interviews, 138–139

D

Damage control, 61–62

Distrust, 29. *See also* passive hostility

Dr. Jekyll/Mr. Hyde, 39–40

E

EAPs. *See* Employee Assistance Programs

Emotional stability, 116

Employee Assistance Programs, 203–206

Enabling, 73–74, 76–77, 79–81, 190; identifying enablers, 140–148

Evaluations: performance appraisal forms, 93–94; skip-level evaluations, 95–98. *See also* feedback

Exit interviews, 135–140

Extraversion, 116

F

Feedback, 77–78, 185–187; 360-degree feedback systems, 95; 360-degree team feedback systems, 131–135; Campbell-Hallam-Team Development Survey (TDS),